MAJOR
Themes
from
MINOR
Prophets

MAJOR
Themes
from
MINOR
Prophets

HARRY YOUNG

AUTUMN

HOUSE

Acknowledgements

The author would like to thank the Revd Robert Amess for his gracious Foreword, and the Revd Michael Costello for his introduction to Autumn House, Mr Ken Harper of the Christian Book Shop, Tolworth, Surbiton, for his special help and encouragement, and Mrs Barbara Young for preparing the MSS on computer.

The author has used the King James Version, Revised Standard Version and the New International Version in different places. However, there are a number of instances where the author has paraphrased a portion of Scripture in order to make the message more intelligible.

ISBN 1 873796 56 0

Published by
Autumn House
Alma Park, Grantham, Lincolnshire,
NG31 9SL, England.

About the author . . .

The Revd Harry Young . . .

. . . trained as a school teacher at Borough Road College, Isleworth (1938-40), where he achieved a distinction in Education and the prize for 'Teacher of the Year'.

After War service he taught in both primary and secondary schools. In 1963, while continuing to serve as head of Religious Studies in a new secondary school, he returned to Birkbeck College as an evening-class undergraduate and obtained a degree in English Literature, History and Theology. However, throughout that time (1947-63) Mr Young was honorary minister in three Baptist churches.

In 1970 he was ordained and went to Kingston Baptist church, as well as continuing in education (half-time) as lecturer/senior lecturer in Religious Education at the Thomas Huxley College, Acton, London. He was also, during that period, examiner and moderator for the Middlesex Examination Board and the Metropolitan Examination Board in Religious Studies. He retired from his teaching post in 1980 and as a Baptist minister in 1987. He continued as associate minister at the Duke Street Baptist church, Richmond (1988-90), and as interim minister at the Oaklands Baptist church, Surbiton (1991-93). During those years, he served as Free Church chaplain in five local hospitals and chaplain to the Christian Businessmen's Association. He has also been three times chaplain to the Mayor of the Royal Borough of Kingston-upon-Thames.

In 1987 Mr Young was honoured with the presidency of the London Baptist Association and, during that time, led a Baptist delegation to the former Soviet Union. He is widely known for his preaching ministry. His previous publications include:

1965 *Morning Worship for Schools* (Ward Lock)
1970 *The Duke Street (Richmond) Story for the Centenary* (Oliphants)
1970 *Roots and Wings* — a prize-winning book (Marshalls)
1992 *The Church in the Market Place* (200th anniversary of the Kingston Baptist church)

Mr and Mrs Young celebrated their golden wedding three years ago. They have three sons and six grandchildren.

MAJOR Themes *from* MINOR Prophets

Foreword

Messages for today's world

FOR MANY CHRISTIANS, the minor prophets are little-known documents, difficult to find, tucked away at the end of the Old Testament. How to find them is a problem, let alone understanding them!

Who were these prophets? Why have their messages been recorded for us? Even to have the answers to some of these questions is but a beginning, for they speak of the Northern Kingdom and the South, of exile and return. Even experienced readers are confused here, as the minor prophets do not appear in chronological order in the biblical canon. Bible history after Solomon is a blur for many.

Unless we know something of the situations that these prophets addressed, what they actually had to say will inevitably be divorced from the context, and that is dangerous. In all these matters Harry Young helps us in a way that is erudite yet accessible.

Though lost in the mists of time, in truth the minor prophets were real people, addressing real situations. Again, like these studies, their work was preached before being written down. Revd Young also addressed a real congregation, and applied his messages to meet real-life problems. In the purposes of God the messages of these prophets have been preserved for us, just as these messages, too, have been committed to print for their preservation, to be appreciated by a wider audience than was originally possible.

Harry Young, treasured and greatly respected by so many in Duke

Street Baptist Church, Richmond, and beyond, first gave these studies as a mid-week series. This is the church with which he has had a lifelong acquaintance and until comparatively recently, as associate pastor. To me, Harry is an honoured colleague, and I have benefited from his lifetime of experience. Still in much demand in the churches, Revd Young has been discovered by many others who recognize a voice for today. It is not surprising then that, as with the original prophecies, here are real messages, addressed to real people, facing real situations. These studies struck a chord and met a need when first delivered; so much so that it was requested that they might be preserved and treasured by a wider audience. They too, like the original prophecies, have been recorded for us to value, digest and profit by, now with the added benefit of questions and points for group discussion.

Here the warmth and wisdom of Harry Young — no minor prophet — come through in his own inimitable way. Here is scholarship, plus the pastor's heart. Here is the wisdom of the prophets applied, essential for all prophecy. Neither the first prophets nor Harry Young were divorced from their time and circumstances, and here are words for today which I most warmly recommend to a wider readership.

REVD ROBERT AMESS, Richmond

Contents

MAJOR
Themes
from
MINOR
Prophets

Introduction

'A legacy of unread books'

The village of Sipson lies just north of the Bath road in Middlesex. It was known as 'the fruity village' because it was surrounded by fertile land producing fine-quality produce for Covent Garden. Just a mile away, however, was the prefabricated airport at Heathrow which mushroomed as the Second World War ended; and, as it inevitably grew and grew, it threatened to spread its tentacles like a giant octopus across the Bath road and envelop the village. The Baptist chapel faced an uncertain future and so the congregation was happy to call a recently-demobbed schoolmaster to be the lay pastor.

In due time the village was transformed, though not quite in the way that everyone expected. The huge runways, built to receive and dispatch the great giants of the airways, did not trespass beyond that ancient coach road, but two beautiful houses were demolished with many others as the character of the village was completely transformed, though the chapel has survived 'until this day'.

It was from one of those houses, 'Hollycroft', that my legacy of books came to me as a young pastor — handsome volumes, theological treasures — and, to my great delight, valuable bookcases accompanied them! As I began to use them, I discovered that many had never been read! The pages were uncut; it needed a sharp knife to open them in order to reveal those otherwise unsearchable riches within.

Much of the Old Testament is like that, and especially the twelve small books which are known as the minor prophets. They are largely unexplored territory, unvisited and uncut! Who were those 'holy men of God who spoke as they were moved by the Holy Spirit'? When did they live and what was their message for the world in which they prophesied? 'Why on earth,' I hear you say, 'are they included in Scripture and how is their message relevant to our world, so vastly different from theirs? Are they still useful for teaching, rebuking, correcting and training in righteousness? Will they "thoroughly equip us for every good work"?'[1]

Let us leave it an open verdict for the moment as I invite you to join me on a journey of exploration, for woven into the tapestry of ancient prophecy we shall discover many surprises. Those were men who 'spoke from God as they were carried away by the Holy Spirit'.[2] They knew anger and frustration, awe and anguish, hope and despair, but they also knew a God of uncompromising holiness, irrevocable justice and inexhaustible love and mercy. We shall need patience and perseverance to reach the heart of the matter. The beginning of our acquaintance with those men of God may only be a definition of our ignorance; at first we may only see through a glass darkly, but if we have the stamina to endure to the end, we shall realize, perhaps as never before, that 'in the past God spoke to our forefathers through the prophets at many times and in various ways.'[3]

When a much-loved man of God arrived for a weekend of ministry at the home of his host, he was shown to his room with the words, 'The Prophet's Chamber, Mr Bird.' It was rather small and unattractive. 'A minor prophet, I presume,' was his unspoken response!

It is more than an affectation of modesty thus to describe myself, but I must acknowledge my deep gratitude to the congregation of the Duke Street Baptist church in Richmond upon Thames, with whom I first shared these studies and who, with characteristic generosity, encouraged me to offer them to others. In celebration of the Revised Standard Version of the Bible in 1952, Canon Briggs wrote these words:

> 'God has spoken by His prophets,
> Spoken His unchanging word,
> Each from age to age proclaiming
> God the one, the righteous Lord.
> In the world's despair and turmoil,
> One firm anchor holding fast,
> God is on His throne eternal,
> He alone, the first and last.'

References:
[1] 2 Tim. 3:16. [2] 2 Peter 1:21. [3] Heb. 1:1.

MAJOR
Themes
from
MINOR
Prophets

Hosea

The prophet of God's unchanging love

A WINDOW ON HOSEA'S TIME

Before we encounter Hosea, the first of the so-called 'minor prophets' of the Old Testament, we need to understand that at this time — in the middle of the eighth century BC — God's chosen people, Israel, were divided unequally into two kingdoms. The two tribes of Judah and Benjamin formed the Southern Kingdom, centred around Jerusalem. The remaining ten tribes formed the Northern Kingdom with Samaria as its capital. The mighty Kingdom of Assyria posed an ever-present threat from the north as Egypt had done in the south.

Hosea was himself a northerner. This was a time of political chaos, of royal assassinations and idolatry. God's people had forsaken their covenant with the true God, despising His steadfast love. They had adopted the false gods of Canaanite religion, especially Baal worship, a fertility cult. It was a time of moral collapse and wickedness.

The sad saga of the nation is mirrored in the tragic circumstances of Hosea's personal story. He is writing under great emotional stress. His prophecy is a vale of tears, but it becomes a valley of hope, even as the weeping, which endures through the night, turns to joy when morning comes. It is a story of unfaithfulness, but it is also a story of amazing grace, unparalleled forgiveness and matchless love.

You will discover, perhaps to your surprise, that Hosea's message, though addressing the specific problems of his own time, is remarkably contemporary and poignantly relevant to the situation of moral decadence and broken relationships in today's world. A heart-rending but beautiful experience awaits you . . . .

'HOSEA, I PRESUME. Glad to meet you!'

As soon as he enters the room of our dark world, we are conscious that Hosea brings with him his own private daylight. He bears the scars of a bruising personal experience, but his face shines with the unchanging love of God.

Here is a man with a story to tell of tragedy and triumph, of hurting and healing, of guilt and grace. We are compelled to sit at his feet and listen.

Hosea is placed first of the twelve minor prophets in the canon of Scripture, the first among equals, even though Amos was before him. As we hear him, we realize how appropriate this seems to be. Amos may preach with sheer objectivity about the social, political and religious crises of the eighth century BC, but Hosea is in the thick of it and so sensitively aware of the tragedy of a people estranged from God, yet he himself is filled with the optimism of grace. No other prophet comes near to the New Testament revelation of God's love; 'a nearer kinsman of Christian evangelists', as someone has said, 'the prophet nearest to Jesus'.

We need to understand how the Kingdom of Israel was divided after the death of Solomon, around 922BC. There were ten tribes in the Northern Kingdom, of which Ephraim was the most prominent and Samaria the capital city. The tribes of Judah and Benjamin formed the Southern Kingdom around Jerusalem. Egypt was the great power to the south, Assyria to the north — Assyria which was to come down 'like a wolf on the fold' and devour the North in a triumphant advance across 'the fertile crescent', as the region is often called.

It is of equal importance to understand the theological background. The great moment of Israel's salvation history was the Exodus, when after deliverance from the slavery of Egypt they entered into a covenant relationship with God, sealed with the Commandments at the holy mountain of Sinai. They were to enjoy a special relationship with God as His people, the object of His steadfast love. In the terms of the covenant, God's people were required to return their love, their loyalty and

17

faithful obedience, as well as their worship, confirmed by inner dispositions of righteousness, and outward personal and social holiness. They were not, however, to be puppets manipulated by invisible hands, but a responsible people who would surely have to live with the consequences of their own decisions.

On Israel's arrival in the Promised Land, they were confronted with the Baal worship of Canaan, a fertility cult in which the god was presented as 'the husband of the land', the giver of corn, oil and wine. Sacrifices in Baal worship were in the nature of appeasement, not atonement, with rituals which included prostitution, idolatry and spiritism. Israel became seriously infected with Baal worship, became apostate and guilty of spiritual adultery. This explains the volcanic eruptions of that indignant servant of God, desperate to warn of an impending catastrophe and of imminent doom, yet stubborn in his refusal to abandon hope.

We know little of Hosea himself. Some have thought he might have been a baker, since he speaks of a heated oven and kneaded dough. Ephraim is a cake not turned — a flat cake not turned over.[1] Was ever an analogy so evocative of a double-dealing, two-timing, half-hearted religion? Others have thought of him as a farmer because of so many agricultural allusions. He was no mere uneducated countryman, however, but an elegant and gifted writer, with a good knowledge of history, a broad grasp of contemporary politics, and a theology with its roots in true worship and its fruits in godly living.

The key which unlocks the treasure chest of Hosea's prophetic ministry is awareness of the fact that the situation in Israel and her broken relationship with God, in all its tragedy and disobedience, is paralleled in his own intimate and private life. It leads him to identify Israel's dilemma of infidelity and describe it in terms of his own heart-break and near despair. It also leads him ever more deeply into the nature of forgiving love, love to the uttermost, a love that never lets go!

Let Hosea himself open that most confidential file and reveal his own experience.

'It was the Lord who told me to take Gomer, a woman of ill-repute, to be my wife. The only explanation I could offer myself for so strange a command was that our marriage was to be a redemptive act — to rescue a defiled and adulterous woman, loose and promiscuous, lift her from the depths of depravity and degradation into which she had fallen, reinstate her in society, and give her respectability and a rebirth into a new relationship and a new family of happiness and love. You will understand it was not an easy option, but if the required obedience was in God's purpose, then so be it. Trusting in God, I obeyed.' All the time, as he speaks with much emotion, we see the picture developing like a negative in the photographer's dark-room.

'We had children, as you would expect,' he continued, 'and God even dictated what their names should be. Strange, I thought, until it dawned on me that since names have meanings, this was yet another way in which God was speaking, when the first boy was born of a bloody purge, the next of a nation "not loved", and then a nation who are "no longer my people". I ought to add (and here we realize Hosea's voice recovers its buoyancy and strength) I absolutely refused to believe that God's people would not be reunited under a new leader, punishment first, yes, but in God's good time, restoration.'

Do we detect tears in the prophet's eyes as he struggles to continue his story? 'You will find it hard to believe this' — he finds it difficult to control his feelings — 'but after all I did for Gomer, all the love and forgiveness I offered her, she deserted me and returned to her evil and depraved ways of immorality and infidelity. I was devastated, distraught and broken. Imagine my dismay and disbelief when I clearly heard the Lord call me once more. "Go, show your love to your wife again." "What — take *her* back again, Lord?" — I rebelled — "the woman whom I rescued from the pit of wickedness and to whom I gave every opportunity to start a new life? You ask too much, Lord, far too much!" But when I heard the Lord say, "Love her as the Lord loves Israel" and I remembered His infinite patience and unquenchable love for His chosen people, I relented. If God can do it, with His help I can do it! By the time I found her, she had become a slave, so depraved and humiliated and so ashamed that although I might have expected to pay thirty shekels of silver to buy her back, she was on offer at half the price!'

Of course, that is only half the story, but sufficient for us to begin to admire the man for his magnanimity and amazing grace. Naturally, Gomer was to be disciplined and put on probation before the sweet intimacies of marriage could be enjoyed once more.

By now we really have arrived at the heart of the matter, because Hosea's story is a parable in action. Israel, chosen by God, so wilful, so disobedient, to whom so much was given, yet so unworthy, so faithless, the people of the covenant are never to be forsaken. The loving God never closes His door, the waiting Father who continuously scans the horizon to catch the first glimpse of a returning prodigal. Israel was not only to be thought of as His bride, but also His child whom He taught to walk and took up in His arms, led with cords of human kindness and ties of love.[2]

As you persevere in reading through the chapters of Hosea's prophecy, you will find oracles which alternate between a demoralized confusion and anxiety and words of supreme tenderness in the call to repentance. There are dire warnings and pronouncements of inevitable judgement, but also the passionate wooings of an undeserving people. There will be suffering in exile for, as we have said, God — even God — cannot do other than allow us to reap the consequences of our own decisions, our deliberate backsliding, but the way back to Him will always be open. Spiritual leaders are condemned for leaving people to die for lack of knowledge, but, at least, the cry of the penitent will be heard again.

'Let us return to the Lord. He will heal us and bind up our wounds; He will revive us, on the third day; He will restore us that we may live in His presence.'[3] It is beautiful Easter language, the vocabulary of resurrection, transporting us in a twinkling of an eye from the Old dispensation to the New, from the Old Covenant to the New Covenant, and from the Old Israel to the New Israel, the Church which is the people of God.

> 'Ransomed, healed, restored, forgiven,
> Who like thee His praise shall sing?'

It was Goethe who once said, 'I never had great suffering but that I made it into a poem.'

This is what Hosea has done in the beauty of his eloquence and the vividness of his metaphors. Nothing is lost in translation in a range of language like that of Milton in his great classic *Paradise Lost*, or the lamentations of King Lear in the Shakespearean tragedy where the despairing father speaks of the marbled-hearted ingratitude of his daughter. If the consequences of unfaithfulness are terrible, the consequences of repentance — forgiveness, healing and reconciliation — are splendid, fragrant and beautiful. Hosea takes us for a walk through the woods of his imagination to see the dew sparkling in the spring sunshine, to inhale the sweet smell of the cedar trees and admire the blossoming lilies as well as the first signs of fruit on the spreading branches of the recently pruned vines. The worship of impotent idols is no more: no more profane human sacrifices, no more waywardness and apostasy, no other God, no other Saviour. We humbly ask for wisdom and discernment to understand that the ways of the Lord are right; the righteous walk in them.

We must now ask what the Lord is saying to us and to our world, no less troubled, wicked and dangerous than the world of the eighth century BC when Hosea lived. Domestic suffering has become almost commonplace in the life of our nation and indeed across the world. There is scarcely a family nowadays which is not touched in some way. It may be a rebellious adolescent, kicking against the pricks, and casting off the restraints of a moral upbringing and searching for the so-called freedom which is so prevalent and popular. It may be an unfaithful husband or wife, a break-up of marriage causing hurt and grief and often adversely affecting innocent children. There must always be a welcome home for the prodigal child whose second thoughts are of true repentance and a deep desire to repair broken relationships. Forgiveness must always be on offer where it is reciprocated with real regret and unqualified resolve. Above all, we need reminding that God's love never changes. He receives us graciously; He who knows our human frailty.

We may also suffer backsliding in our own personal spiritual life. We may lose our first love and in our lukewarmness fall away; but we only need to hear the knock on the door, and when we hear the unmistakable voice of the Lord, open it, invite Him in and spread the table of communion.

We may experience bereavement, redundancy, adversity; we can become demoralized and disillusioned. On the other hand, we may become trapped in a system of materialism, preoccupied with prosperity, affluence and love of the world. God is unchanging in His steadfast love: His compassion never fails, a compassion we, too, need to emulate when confronted by the casualties of this world, a compassion which feels the pain when someone else is hurting.

Two men, as they left the church, looked up to the weather-vane on top of the steeple on which were the words, 'God is Love'.

'I suppose that means that God's love changes with the wind?' said one.

'Oh, no,' the other replied, 'that means God is Love, whichever way the wind blows.'

The message of Hosea is surely this: that in the end we can rejoice in the triumph of love and the victory of faith that overcomes the world.

The apostle John closely resembles Hosea, as is revealed in his letters. He speaks of fellowship with God the Father, a faithful and just God, ready to forgive our sins and purify us from all unrighteousness. 'God is Love' is never a cliché, never a slogan, but Calvary-flavoured, a deep, deep love which paid the supreme sacrifice on the cross.

George Matheson, at a time of extreme mental stress, wrote a hymn which was, he said, 'the fruit of pain'. Perhaps the cause was his blindness or an unrequited love. Hosea would have loved these words:

> 'O Love that will not let me go,
> I rest my weary soul in Thee;
> I give Thee back the life I owe,
> That in Thine ocean depths its flow
> May richer, fuller be.'

We, too, may see the 'rainbow through the rain', the symbol of God's faithfulness, its span between heaven and earth reminding us that our hopes for the future are founded on God's grace. We may also see the 'red blossoms' that spring from sacrifice, a tearless morn and endless life.

Let the apostle John, who knew the loneliness of exile and the pain of undeserved suffering, have the last word. He ends his first letter like this:

'Jesus Christ is the true God. Dear children, keep yourselves from false idols.'

Hosea would have said 'Amen' to that!

---

[1] Hosea 7:4, 7. [2] Hosea 11:1-4, [3] Hosea 6:1-3.

HOSEA: STUDY GUIDE

For personal reflection and/or group discussion

1. How and why did Israel become infected with Baal worship?
    What are the 'idols' people worship nowadays?

2. Hosea is described as 'the prophet nearest to Jesus'. What features in
    Hosea's character do you most admire?

3. How can this prophecy be used in situations of domestic strife and
    suffering in today's world?

4. How can Hosea's story help to restore someone whom we might
    describe as a 'backslider'?

5. Recall the words of Goethe (in the text):
    'I never had great suffering but that I made it into a poem.'

    Think of any experience of suffering — loss, bereavement — in your life
    and try to write a poem about it.

6. Dr Billy Graham once said:
    'In these days of guilt complexes, perhaps the most glorious word in the
    English language is forgiveness.' A lovely thought, but are there no limits
    to forgiveness? Does 'seventy times seven' mean that there are none?
    (See Matthew 18:21, 22.)

    and *finally*
    'Love changes everything,
    How I tremble at your name.
    Nothing in the world will ever be the same.'
    — (from 'Aspects of Love' by Andrew Lloyd Webber)

MAJOR
Themes
from
MINOR
Prophets

Amos

*The prophet
of social
justice*

A WINDOW ON AMOS' TIME

Our encounter with Hosea may have been a rather sentimental journey, a meeting with a man of sorrows, acquainted with grief, the story of a personal tragedy as well as that of a national crisis. We must now prepare ourselves for a very different experience . . . .

We are to meet Amos; and we must be careful not to underestimate him. A son of the soil he may be, but we shall find him to be a formidable character, a man who lived by the spiritual and moral principles enshrined in the special relationship he enjoyed with God.

Amos belonged to the southern kingdom in the middle of the eighth century BC; a shepherd who also grew figs and was enterprising enough to travel up to Bethel in the Samaritan north to sell his produce. Here he saw the luxurious life-style of a favoured few who, with unscrupulous and callous wickedness and greed, oppressed the poor. He saw the idolatry and the moral depravity which went with it. He saw corruption and, in his anger and with unexpected eloquence, he condemned the guilty and passionately cried out for righteousness and social justice. Amos sensed the danger Israel was in, long before the crisis came with the Assyrian conquest. But his dire warnings went unheeded. His hope, however, was never extinguished as, in the far future, he believed that 'the kingdom shall be the Lord's'.

In another adventure, prepare to be astonished at the powerful relevance of this ancient prophet who still speaks in our day to our world. He should, indeed, be living at this hour!

IT WAS THE Lakeland poet William Wordsworth who, in 1802, wrote a sonnet in praise of John Milton, the great Puritan writer:

> 'Milton! Thou should'st be living at this hour;
> England hath need of thee; she is a fen
> Of stagnant waters; altar, sword and pen,
> Fireside, the heroic wealth of hall and bower,
> Have forfeited their ancient English dower
> Of inward happiness, We are selfish men;
> Oh! raise us up, return to us again;
> And give us manners, virtue, freedom, power.'

When I contemplate our world as it is today, and in particular our own country where irreligion, excessive individualism and rising crime, not to mention political confusion, are features of an ever increasingly decadent society, I should like to attribute the poet's words to another of the prophets of the eighth century BC. His name is Amos — a name that might well be also an acronym for a Man of Strength, a Man of Spirituality, a Man of Social Justice.

Come with me for a walk in the wild wilderness of Tekoa; it isn't far from Jerusalem. I have arranged for us to meet Amos. He advised me to be precise about the time and place, else we might never see him. You may hear a lion roar, but do not be afraid; you may see an eagle swoop upon its innocent and unguarded prey. You may hear the soft breeze in the sycamore and fig trees and even the sound of music of the rolling river or never-failing stream. If darkness should fall, Amos is sure to urge us to look up to the sky, for the starry universe above, like the moral law within, speaks to him of the One whose name is Lord.

Do not expect to see him dressed as a rabbi or a Levite; he is a shepherd and a dresser of fig trees, but do not underestimate him. He has an eye to business and makes frequent journeys up country to Samaria and Bethel (where the money is) to sell his wool and fruit. In fact, it was at Bethel where the King's chaplain — of all people — so disliked his blunt warnings of imminent judgement that he ordered him out.

'Go back where you came from, you silly old fool; do your doom and gloom stuff down there and leave us alone!' I paraphrase, of course!

It was with humility and yet with holy boldness that Amos replied: 'I'm neither a prophet nor do I belong to a prophet's family. I'm just a herdsman; I grow figs. It was no other than the Lord who called me to leave my sheep and preach to Israel, and you had better listen to what the Lord told me to say!'

You will remember how the Kingdom of Israel was divided after the death of Solomon. There was Judah to which Amos belonged, and Israel, then seriously threatened by the rising power of Assyria. The prophet had a solemn word for Judah and other adjacent peoples, but it was to Israel, the Northern Kingdom, to whom he was chiefly sent. He had keenly observed the situation there. There was much wealth and prosperity, a handsome revenue from tolls extracted from passing traders; there were money-lenders, heartless sharks oppressing the poor without mercy; bribery and corruption were rampant. The rich were living in luxury, while the poor could scarcely afford a pair of shoes or a covering to keep them warm at night; their overcoats had gone to the pawnbroker! There was a shallow veneer of religion, empty rituals of sacrifices and tithes, but no inward dispositions of righteousness. Their covenant relationship with the Lord was broken and profaned by gross immorality and promiscuity. The few lived in idleness, with an abundance of wine and fine food, homes for the winter and summer. Amos saw all that with his own eyes and burned with a passion for morality, righteousness and social justice. He could not hold his peace; such was the wickedness of an apostate Israel that judgement must come. There was no hiding place from God's anger, no escape. God's law could not be broken with impunity, but there was room for repentance and a constant invitation to return to His love; there was the hope of restoration, however far in the future it might be.

It was psychologically shrewd of Amos to speak out first against Israel's neighbours, who, though they were without the law, transgressed against the law written on their hearts as witnessed by their consciences, often spoken of as 'the voice of God'. Those people were guilty of cruelty, slave trading, hate, atrocities against pregnant women, and desecration of the dead. When Amos turned his vehement eloquence upon Judah, the people of Bethel might even have applauded, for there was no love lost between Samaria and Jerusalem. However, when he turned his fire of condemnation upon Israel, he was met only with anger and derision.

By now we have met with Amos at the agreed place. We are impressed with his rustic simplicity. His simple faith is that of a man who lives close to nature, where, in the quiet pastures, he can clearly hear the still small voice of the Lord.

What he heard was no surprise. He had — farmer-cum-commercial traveller — seen the evils in Israel for himself . . . .

'I knew it was the Lord calling me,' Amos begins his story, 'Why me? I asked myself. I felt so inadequate, so ill-equipped, until I realized that if God commanded, I had to obey. God would tell me what to say. I reminded Israel of their history, the wonderful deliverance from Egypt's bondage in the Exodus and the solemn covenant into which their ancestors had freely entered at Sinai. They were the people of God. Had they totally forgotten the commandments and did they not realize that the blessings of obedience had vanished? Punishment would be swift and sure. They had been chosen of all the families of the earth; so great a privilege, so great a responsibility, so triumphant a victory at the Red Sea, so deep a tragedy of the increasing sinfulness of a broken trust. I told them they had spurned the word of the Lord and failed miserably to keep His commandments. What broke my heart (here Amos, like Hosea, can scarcely hold back the tears of disappointment and despair) was that I knew that Samaria would be destroyed, beautiful houses destroyed, only traces left to show posterity they once existed, and the population taken into exile to be lost for ever!'

We may now imagine that Amos begs to be excused — there is work to do — but perhaps we might like a copy of his manuscript, for he had written it all down for future generations to read. We are deeply moved by his words, often ironic and bitter, but also profound and beautiful.

'Prepare to meet thy God' we read, and he describes his early warnings of coming judgement. He warns of famine, withered crops in rainless fields, plagues of locusts like those which afflicted the Egyptians; but, he adds, 'yet you have not returned to Me.' God is Almighty, the Great Creator, the God of power, of transcendent majesty, a God of holiness: 'the quality that makes God what He is'; whereas Israel is like a fallen virgin, raped, ravaged and deserted with no one to lift her up. 'Seek the Lord and live,' he cries. 'Seek the Lord; hate evil.' His lamentations are interwoven with his prayers as Amos intercedes, like Abraham pleading for Sodom, that God will show mercy if the people show true repentance. He is, however, met with complacency, indifference and derision; even those who can, in their wisdom, read the signs of the times are too frightened to open their mouths. Amos speaks plainly of the inevitable consequences of Israel's sin: their cities will be destroyed and the people taken away into exile. Their false sense of security will be shattered; their arrogance and pride will dissolve in abject humiliation. The day of the Lord will be a day of darkness 'without a ray of brightness'.

When a distinguished minister completed a series of studies on the prophet Amos at the Keswick Convention more than twenty years ago, the rumour flew around that, by then, even Amos was saying that he was sorry he had written the book in the first place! You may be feeling like that, rather as you do when you cannot take any more bad news, reach for your remote control and switch off the television, or search the channels for something more agreeable, but let me encourage you to endure to the end. Two travellers, one a veteran and the other a novice, were climbing in the Pyrenees. Darkness compelled them to sleep on a ledge. Towards morning a storm came up and a howling wind that wailed fiercely among the heights. The frightened novice woke his friend and said, 'I think it is the end of the world!'

'Oh, no,' said his companion, 'this is how the dawn comes to the Pyrenees!'

Amos can reach beyond the horizon of doom and disaster with the belief that this dark and stormy night of Divine retribution will yield to a new dawn of restoration, prosperity and security. But first we must brace ourselves to hear more from this shepherd-preacher, this prophet of justice who is as uncompromising in his condemnation of hypocrisy and perverted worship as he is unswerving in his support of righteousness. He sees visions of the coming catastrophe, even as he dreams of future glory. He sees yet another plague of locusts devouring every green thing, and a drought which scorches the land. He then sees the Lord appearing as a master-builder, with a plumb-line in his hand. Here we are on more familiar ground, with the picture of a homely, frequently improvised gadget we use to prove the true and perpendicular. It is held against the crumbling wall of Israel's civilization, built as it is on corrupt and rotten foundations. A basket of ripe summer fruit then comes into his vision and the prophet has no doubt as to its meaning: Israel is ripe for destruction. We must excuse the prophet's monotonous repetitions; they are the evidence of the anguish in his heart as he contemplates the inevitable result of their evil ways. There will be a famine in the land, and not only for food and drink, but a famine for the Word of God.

Now that we have opened up the pages of this remarkable, relevant little book, we must ask what message does Amos have for our world and for our nation, what message for us?

There is a spiritual hunger everywhere, another kind of famine. Politicians and prelates alike do not seem to have the answer to the ever-declining standards in relationship and behaviour. The men at the Dispatch Box seem only to exchange arid and ritualistic arguments of exaggerations and contradictions, and the men in the pulpit speak often with an uncertain sound. Morality is the principle on which our world depends; social justice must be a priority for us all, yet in our topsy-turvy world we must not be overcome by the darkness. We must respond to God's call to be a visible as well as a vocal witness to the truth, refusing to be conformed to this world and squeezed into its image, but always responding to human need with compassion and care. At a time when so many are disillusioned with our world, we must always bring a message of hope and highlight the goodness all around us when only slander and sleaze steal the headlines.

The spirit of Amos is reflected strongly by James in his New Testament letter, so renowned for its practical emphasis of the Christian faith. James urged us to take as an example those prophets who spoke in the name of the Lord. In his call for steadfastness, James urged his reader to turn from jealousy and self-aggrandizement and 'to show his works in the meekness of wisdom'.

The message of Amos lives on as we proclaim a message of righteousness, temperance and judgement, and practise a ministry of healing and reconciliation. When God has spoken through His Word, we dare not be silent. 'Prepare to meet thy God', the clarion call of Amos, is a word of warning, but we may also see it as a word of welcome, as in repentance and faith we make ready to meet the Lord.

AMOS: STUDY GUIDE

For personal reflection and/or group discussion

1. Do you think that people who live in the countryside are more 'spiritual' than people who live in the city? Give reasons for your answer.

2. If Amos were alive today, do you think he would make a good politician? What issues would concern him most?

3. That great archbishop, William Temple, once said:
    'It is a mistake to say that God is only interested in religion.'
    What do you think he meant?

4. Do you see conflict between 'the social gospel' and 'the spiritual gospel'?
    Or are they complementary; two faces of the same Gospel?

5. How could you use Amos' vision of the man with the plumb-line when sharing the Gospel today? (Amos 7:7-9.)

6. Are there similarities between the preaching of Amos and the teaching of James in his practical, New Testament letter?

7. 'The Christian faith requires us to have sensitivity to social need, injustice and oppression.' What organizations can you recommend who are meeting this requirement?

MAJOR
Themes
from
MINOR
Prophets

Micah

The prophet of Messianic hope

A WINDOW ON MICAH'S TIME

The eighth century BC was a dark time in the history of God's people Israel. It was a time of apostasy and a broken covenant; a time of injustice, of the exploitation of the poor, and of rampant corruption. But the darkness was illuminated by men of God who spoke with passion to denounce idolatry, immorality and other evils. Yet with the same energy and eloquence these prophets expounded what is the quintessence of true religion, that is the inspired behaviour of those who fear God, obey His commandments and walk in His ways. They also spoke with an unquenchable optimism and an undimmed hope that righteousness would eventually triumph in the new dawn of God's kingdom.

Having encountered Hosea and Amos, we are eager to meet Micah. He was a countryman from Judah who, living at the end of the eighth century before Christ, might well have known them. He certainly knew and greatly admired Isaiah whom he sought to emulate. It was said of Isaiah, 'He had a mouth of gold with morning in his eyes' — elegant if rather extravagant words which are also true of Micah.

Micah had a good grasp of the contemporary situation politically but, surprisingly for a farmer, he was profoundly conversant with the ethics of religion and those inward dispositions which are the outward evidence of true faith.

You are now invited to become something of an astronomer, to scan the dark historical sky and see stars — which, for those who love alliteration (and most preachers do!) I have named as power, peace, prophecy, personal religion and pardon. You may even feel as did John Keats when he first looked into Chapman's Homer:

> 'Then felt I like some watcher in the skies
> When a new planet swims into his ken'!

Micah demanded that the people listen to what the Lord says. He still does!

MAY WE CLOSE our eyes and use our imagination? We are in the depths of the countryside. It is night and all is silent. Above us is the inky blackness of the dark sky; but as we look up we can see five bright, shining stars. We sit in the darkness and listen!

That is the picture of the prophecy of Micah: words of judgement upon Israel, vivid oracles of doom and gloom to which we are becoming accustomed in these studies. However, in the midst of his moods of despair and messages of judgement, there are five of the choicest passages in all Scripture, five stars, becoming light in the darkness, five great words of hope, deliverance, revival and restoration.

Micah was a country man like Amos, whom he might have known, a man of humble origins. He lived in Moresheth, about twenty-five miles south-west of Jerusalem in the fertile region of the Shephelah (or Lowlands) of Judah, well known for its green and fertile fields and olive groves. He was contemporary with Isaiah of Jerusalem who was an aristocrat and a man about court, whereas Micah was a peasant farmer, but yet a forceful, distinguished man of God.

It was towards the end of the eighth century BC that the word of the Lord came to Micah and with the message the courage and power to proclaim it. His name means 'Who is like the Lord?', which could scarcely be more appropriate for a man who spoke with righteous indignation because of the evils all around him, and yet expounded the meaning of the true religion as few others had done before him. The Lord was his light which no darkness could overcome; the Lord was his confidence which no evil could destroy; the Lord was his hope which nothing could remove.

After Solomon died, Israel was partitioned into two kingdoms, Judah and Israel. Jerusalem, the city set upon a hill, could not hide its prestige and pride for there was the temple as the centre of its worship. Samaria as the capital of the Northern Kingdom provided an alternative focus of worship, but had become a centre of idolatry and false religion. The awesome shadow of Assyria lay across the land, an ever-present threat to Israel which prophets, including Micah, so clearly saw.

Micah shares the grief of God as he surveys the contemporary scene. He sees through the formalities of religion and is sensitive to its contradictions. His sympathies are with the poor who are exploited and often dispossessed by those for whom wealth is power and money a god. The people of God are in breach of their special covenant relationship, breaking the commandments and forgetting the saving acts of God as in the Exodus. Micah sees the priests and prophets as corrupt, embracing the false gods of the Canaanite religion which was always accompanied by social injustice, witchcraft and gross immorality, a religion polluted and without righteousness; in brief, a shame and a sham. He tries to control his emotions, and through his tears he cries out again and again, 'Listen to what the Lord says.'

His message is sombre, for judgement is inevitable. There is no hope for the Northern Kingdom. Samaria will surely fall to the might of Assyria. Jerusalem may have a brief respite; the Assyrian army will reach no further than the gates of Jerusalem, but later the city will fall to another enemy and many will go into exile.

It is no surprise that such preaching is very unpopular and great efforts are made to silence him. 'Do not preach such things,' they say. 'God is far too patient and kind to do as you say.' Micah, however, knows the sort of preachers they prefer, those who preach about wine and strong drink, when they are well fed and well paid! It is in the midst of this darkness that the first of our five stars appears, because in contrast to the false prophets whom he mocks for their greed and hypocrisy he speaks with humility of himself. 'As for me, I am filled with power, with the spirit of the Lord, and with justice and might.'[1] I wonder if the Apostle Paul had Micah in mind when he charged Timothy to be urgent to preach the word and warned of a time when people would have 'itching ears', turning away from the truth to teachers 'to suit their own likings'.[2]

We know that Micah's words were well remembered long after his death, and were quoted in the Royal Court and saved the prophet Jeremiah from certain death.[3]

As we watch the sky, our second star is visible, the Star of Peace to the World.[4] The words, among the loveliest in the Bible, are Isaiah's words.[5] They speak of the triumph of the Messianic Kingdom over all the world, the uninterrupted peace and harmony of the millennium and of the new Jerusalem, where pilgrims of all nations will come to be taught God's ways and how to walk in them. Micah had a great admiration for Isaiah and was so impressed by the words that he asked permission to use them in his own prophecy! I remember looking up at a giant poster in the former Soviet Union, proclaiming peace to the world. When I asked Galena, our guide, to translate the words for me, she replied, 'It's just an old quotation. It says, "They shall beat their swords into ploughshares."' She did not know that the words were those of Micah in the Bible! It was ironic that these wonderful words of peace should have been so proudly displayed by an 'evil empire', then so arrogant about its military strength.

However, it is the brightest star which now comes into view. Micah has preached about judgement and predicted the exile in Babylon, but he adds, without pausing for breath, 'You will be rescued; the Lord will redeem you.' Who knows the thoughts of the Lord or who can understand His plan? His answer is the glorious promise of the Advent: the Messiah, the future Ruler of Israel, who will surely come. Bethlehem, in the land of Judah, that unlikely and rather insignificant village where King David was born, would be the birthplace of the Messiah.[6] When Herod enquired of the wise men where Christ was to be born, they remembered Micah's words. Later, when at the Feast of Tabernacles people asked if Jesus was 'that prophet'[7] they, too, remembered He had come not originally from Galilee, but Bethlehem, the village where David was born. How wonderful that so many centuries before the Holy birth, Micah saw that the Christ was the hope of the world!

There is deep pathos in the way Micah reveals the grieving heart of God. He is like the parent in distress over a rebellious child, for whom so much has been sacrificed. 'What have I done to deserve all this?' God seems to say[8] 'Have you forgotten the deliverance of your forefathers from bondage in Egypt?' Do His saving acts mean nothing? What is it that God really desires in return for His steadfast love? He certainly does not want extravagant sacrifices, not exaggerated worship, emphatically not human sacrifices. Micah knows the heart of God and offers the finest guide to practical religion in Holy Scripture: 'What does the Lord require from His people?'[9] . . . 'to do justly,.to love mercy and to walk humbly with God.' The cry for justice still rises from all parts of the world, justice for the underprivileged, for those who suffer at the hands of those who use savage and violent but sometimes more subtle means of hurting their fellow human beings. The cry for mercy is also heard, the quality which is twice-blessed, blessed to those who receive it and those who bestow it. Walking humbly with God is a truly marvellous image which occurs throughout the Scripture and speaks of fellowship and communion, unity of purpose and a common destination. When a former president of the United States was sworn in on the lawn of the White House, he opened a Bible at Micah's prophecy and read aloud these splendid words, so sufficient a summary of a godly life.

In the final chapter of his prophecy, Micah looks again at the evil all around him. He is at his wits' end, in great stress and despair. Is there no one who is righteous? People no longer trust one another, not family, neighbour, or friend. Even families are in conflict, words remembered by Jesus who must have felt like Micah as He wept over Jerusalem, not only because He was rejected, but because He foresaw the disasters which lay ahead. Micah seems suddenly to recover his composure: 'I will look to the Lord,' he soliloquizes. 'I will wait for the God of my salvation.'[10]

We shall end as we began and sit in the darkness with Micah. We hear him speak: 'The Lord will be a light to me. He will bring me forth to the light; I will see His righteousness.' We look up into the sky and see another beautiful star, shining as a diamond. What a marvellous way to end with unforgettable words that celebrate God's grace! 'Who is a pardoning God like You' he cries in words of wonder and worship, 'a God who is not forever angry, a God of steadfast love, a God of compassion and faithfulness?' So he celebrates the ultimate victory of righteousness.

As we reflect again on this remarkable book, we see how relevant it is to our world. We despair of human nature; we are overwhelmed by the evil we see around us. We are appalled by our godless society and often dismayed that the Church still seems so divided and ineffective. But this is not the whole story. There is light in the darkness; there are stars still shining in the sky. We must continue to proclaim the beautiful logic of the Christian faith and challenge our generation to grasp what is at the heart of true religion. We must pledge our support for those who work so tirelessly for justice, we must pray for those who dedicate their lives to alleviate the sufferings of others, the victims of poverty, oppression and war. We must seek to live in holiness as we wait for the coming of the day of God, for the new heaven and the new earth where righteousness dwells.

---

[1] Micah 3:8. [2] 2 Tim. 4:2, 3. [3] Micah 3:12; Jer. 26:18. [4] Micah 4:1-3. [5] Isa. 2:1-4. [6] Matt. 2:6. [7] John 7:40. [8] Micah 6:1-5. [9] Micah 6:6-8. [10] Micah 7:7.

MICAH: STUDY GUIDE
For personal reflection and/or group discussion

1. God was surely speaking to His people Israel, denouncing the evils of the day, but equally calling for repentance and a return to righteous living. What is God saying to our generation?

2. Micah's words (see Micah 6:8) have been described as 'the greatest saying in the Old Testament'.
    If you agree, try to say why.
    If you disagree, can you quote other Old Testament words that are equally great or greater?

3. The priests and scribes in Jerusalem knew Micah's prophecy concerning the birth of Jesus in Bethlehem (see Matt. 2:5, 6).
    Do you think they were equally familiar with Micah's message as a whole?

4. Which of the five stars in Micah's dark sky shines most brightly for you?

5. In view of Micah's strongly-ethical emphasis, do you think the Church has paid too much attention to forms of worship and theological arguments and not enough to life-style?
    In what ways does how we behave relate to what we believe?

MAJOR
Themes
from
MINOR
Prophets

Jonah

The reluctant prophet of resurrection and mission

A WINDOW ON JONAH'S TIME

What is your reaction as we reach the story of Jonah? 'At last, this is a prophet I know something about'? It is a story we may have known from childhood, a wondrous tale indeed. Is it no more than an ancient myth, an allegory or parable, or is this an historical narrative for literal interpretation, a miraculous event well within the power and providence of God?

We must not allow the stress of endless argument to deprive us of the real meaning and message of this remarkable book. We need to think deeply, because it will teach us much about the character of God, His righteous anger and yet His infinite compassion and tenderness. It has much to say about 'the wideness in God's mercy' and 'the kindness of His justice', challenging the false limits of our own.

There is, of course, no doubt that Jonah was one of the prophets of the eighth century before Christ. It may be that Jonah wrote the story himself, a self-portrait; or else it is the work of someone else who was familiar with this amazing narrative. Whichever way it was, we not only learn about God's character, but we see ourselves. How often are we unwilling to do what is clearly God's will until He speaks to us 'a second time'?

Someone described the book as 'one of the noblest missionary appeals ever written', but the fact that the revelation of God was for all humanity and that God's love was for all the world, is a lesson Israel never seemed to learn. She abandoned global mission and retreated into exclusivism and squalid isolation. The Church must not fall asleep in a ship of comfort and convenience, dreaming of her private enjoyment of God's grace, while the world is perishing and modern Ninevites need to hear the call to repentance . . . .

'AND NOW FOR something completely different!' That well-worn cliché from the world of broadcasting is particularly apt as we turn to Jonah, the eight-century prophet whose story everybody knows. Children are fascinated by it, as are disbelieving adults who enjoy it as a marvellous piece of fun and fantasy, an ancient parable which loses none of its appeal, however frequently it is told. Fact or fiction, history or folk tale? The debate is endless. Everybody knew the story at the time of Jesus, as Josephus testifies in his *Antiquities of the Jews*: then it was accepted as historical. Our Lord Himself used the story as a warning to an evil generation which needed to repent as much as the ancient Assyrians,[1] but also as a sign of His own resurrection, adding credibility to its historical character.[2]

However, to know the story of 'Jonah and the whale', as it is commonly — and incorrectly — known, is one thing. To know the significance of the book and the man at the centre of the drama is quite another. We still need to open up the pages to see how a man of God is further educated in self-knowledge as well as knowing the gracious God who is merciful and slow to anger, abounding in steadfast love. In this process we may discover surprising things about ourselves. 'I am Jonah' was the way a London preacher described himself as he embarked on a comprehensive study of this unique piece of Old Testament literature.

Jonah was a man of Galilee, from Gath-hepher, about an hour's walk from Nazareth. His name is said to mean 'dove', sometimes used as a symbol of Israel in the Old Testament and a symbol of the Holy Spirit in the New Testament. There is evidence that he had become a popular preacher, a man with quite a charisma, powerful, persuasive and well able to please his audience,[3] as when he prophesied the restoration of the borders of Israel in the days of Jeroboam II. They were welcome words when they were uttered; and when they were fulfilled they greatly boosted the ego of that remarkable man. It explains why Jonah was so much concerned for his reputation, jealous of his success and afraid of failure. We cannot be sure whether the book of Jonah is by an anonymous author, or whether it was written by the man himself in the third person.

God called Jonah to go to Nineveh — that great city of the Assyrians notorious for its wickedness — and preach against it. His face fell; his fluency melted away. That was not a task he relished at all. As he considered it — to deliver an ultimatum which was not only a message of judgement but a call to repentance — he could envisage the Ninevites' giving up their evil ways and their violence, in which case God Himself would repent and the calamity would be averted. His displeasure was quickly followed by his disobedience. He rose to flee from the presence of the Lord. The prophet in his haste must have had a bout of amnesia, for, as we shall discover, he knew the Psalms well. He had, however, forgotten these words:

> 'Where can I go from your spirit?
> Where can I flee from your presence?
> If I make my bed in the depths, you are there.'[4]

He could scarcely believe his good fortune, for on his arrival at the port of Joppa, there, as if waiting, was a ship bound for Tarshish, the furthermost place the prophet could imagine, at the far end of the Great Sea. The fare was promptly paid, which ensured the prophet a warm welcome aboard, and in no time at all Jonah was below deck and fast asleep.

In the brief calm before the storm, we need to reflect that there are times in our lives when we are confronted with a task we would rather not do, a situation we would not wish to face, a person we would rather not meet, a truth we would prefer not to reveal. Just a little prejudice here, a little cowardice there, and we try to escape! More seriously, when God's will for us has been made perfectly plain, we are disobedient. We must not be deceived by circumstances of convenience. Our 'ship to Tarshish' may turn out to be a short cut to disappointment and disaster.

All was calm and bright as the ship weighed anchor and set sail to the west, but before long, dark clouds swept across the sky; a gale-force wind suddenly arose and huge waves began to threaten to break up the vessel. The frightened crew off-loaded the cargo, and, decent and devout men as they were, they cried out in prayer to their gods. 'Who is responsible for this calamity?' they asked one another, while the captain roused the sleeping prophet with a rebuke and a challenge. 'Get up and start praying before we all perish in the storm!' he shouted.

They then decided to cast lots, but it may have been little more than a formality; they knew in their hearts that the fugitive prophet was the man who was the cause. There was no time to answer their questions. As the sea got rougher, the sailors became more and more terrified. 'I'm a Hebrew. I worship the God who *made* the sea,' confessed Jonah; and when in desperation they asked what they should do to him to quieten the sea and save the ship and the lives of all on board, Jonah, now resigned to his fate, replied, 'Throw me in the sea and it will be calm; it's all my fault. I'm so sorry!' The men were sorry also; and it was their turn to be reluctant and unwilling to obey; but after heroic but vain efforts to reach the shore, and absolving themselves of all guilt for what they were about to do, they threw the prophet overboard. The raging sea grew calm at once; the awestruck mariners fell down in worship before the Lord; but what about Jonah? The God of power is also the God of providence: Jonah is buried at sea in the strangest sepulchre of all time — the belly of a great fish!

Near-death experiences have their own fascination, but none is more remarkable than Jonah's. In the very heart of the sea, the currents swirling around him, his head entangled in seaweed, in his distress he cried out to the Lord, 'Save me.' His life seemed to be ebbing away, until he came to terms with his strange environment and realized that he was indeed alive. His prayer was full of echoes of praise and thanksgiving. He repeated his vows and cried out, 'Salvation comes from the Lord.' That was too much for the fish! It was the moment of resurrection for Jonah.

Never was dry land more welcome to fugitive feet than that

unspecified shore on which Jonah found himself. We can only imagine what state he was in! We can only hope he found himself not too far from home, where a hot bath and fresh clothes were available to make the prophet presentable again! No sooner had he recovered his composure and remembered the vows he promised to fulfil, than once again the word of the Lord came to him: 'Arise, go to Nineveh and proclaim the message I gave you.' This time there is obedience, qualified perhaps, and hesitant, but unavoidable. How often God speaks to us a second time! How often He brings us through a traumatic experience to teach us truths we can learn in no other way! The chastening is grievous, but afterwards, in the words of Scripture, it yields the fruits of righteousness.

We may picture Jonah rehearsing the message God gave him, or half of it, as he approached the great sprawling city. 'Yet forty days and Nineveh will be overthrown.' That was the part of the message the prophet heartily approved of, judgement, destruction. The messenger liked the sombre sound of a sermon without salvation. No call to repentance is recorded, but the Ninevites realized that, within the time appointed the opportunity to repent and so avert the catastrophe did exist.

In this incredible story there is yet another miracle which astounded Jonah as much as it amazes us. The people did not laugh and have him in derision. They believed him. His words were like sparks that lit the fire of sudden repentance everywhere. Sackcloth was ordered for all to wear, none excluded, and when the King heard the news it was sackcloth and ashes at once. And there is more: he proclaimed a decree that all should fast, give themselves to prayer and give up their violence and wickedness. 'Perhaps God will change His mind, relent and show compassion and we shall not perish after all!'

The effect of Jonah's preaching defies analysis. Had his arrival coincided with a time of national crisis, or of economic disaster? Were consciences already stirred? What was it that produced that fantastic reaction of repentance and amendment of life? We need to think deeply and look below the surface.

In its brevity, Scripture does not stay to tell the whole story. As we try to unravel the mystery it may be that words of Jesus will help us once more. 'Jonah was a sign to the Ninevites,' He said.[5] At the time, the increasing crowds surrounding Jesus wanted some spectacular proof that He was the Messiah, God's messenger, as He claimed to be. When scribes and Pharisees asked for a sign on another occasion to which we have already referred, Jesus was more specific in His reply. '"As Jonah was three days and three nights in the belly of a huge fish, so the Son of Man will be three days and three nights in the heart of the earth."'[6]

There would seem to be no other conclusion than this: Jonah must have spoken of his entombment in that great creature of the sea and of his survival. It was the living miracle that stood before them that helped to make his message credible. Jesus saw the sign of Jonah as the most powerful sign to be offered to the world, His own death and resurrection. There is a word for us also, because the most convincing argument for the truth of the Christian Gospel is surely the observable transformations in the lives of those who believe it and share it with others. It is the new life in Christ which is expressed so beautifully in our baptism, and which is the most compelling evidence of God's grace in our lives.

Jonah's anger is not concealed. He does not yet understand that God's repentance means that His mercy and compassion are perfectly blended with His righteousness and justice. Where repentance and faith are verified by amendment of lifestyle, a new way of life in conformity with God's laws, there is salvation. The sulking prophet has still much to learn about God's character. He seeks to justify his initial hasty disobedience as if he knew what God would do. He could not bear the thought of returning home. How much more would he have preferred to boast, 'I prophesied and it came to pass'? He would rather die than go home and tell them that Nineveh was not destroyed after all.

How gentle and patient God is with His stubborn prophet

who retreats to the treeless plain on the east side of the city, still refusing to believe that God will not destroy it. In the hot sun he is in much discomfort. Eventually the flimsy shade he had managed to provide himself with was improved by the swift and sudden growth of a strange plant. Its broad leaves gave Jonah just a little happiness in the midst of his depression — but not for long.

At dawn, much to his chagrin, the vulnerable plant was attacked by a worm or a host of caterpillar-like insects and destroyed. Jonah was plunged into deeper despair as the east wind blew and the sun blazed down on the hapless, fainting prophet. The dialogue with which the story ends is most moving . . . .

He is angry — enough to die — full of pity for the plant. 'How much more,' says God, 'ought I to be concerned about this great city, with its huge population, including thousands of young children, not to mention the animals.' The story ends abruptly. It has been suggested that the abrupt end means that, Third Person notwithstanding, it was Jonah who wrote it after all — in sackcloth and ashes! At least, as David Kossoff would say, Jonah got the point!

There are those who claim that the book was written to show that Israel had a mission for the world and to be a light to lighten the Gentiles; that the chosen ones were not to privatize the Good News, but share it with all men.

There is a message for the Church of today. The Gospel must not remain within the four walls of a place of worship. We are not called to be once-a-week-pew-warmers. Rather we must move out into the community with compassion and under-standing, to meet felt needs, to plead for justice, truth and goodness.

One greater than Jonah calls us a second time . . . may we be able to say with the Apostle Paul, '"I was not disobedient to the Heavenly vision . . . I preached that the Gentiles should re-pent and turn to God, and prove their repentance by their deeds."'[7]

If we share the Gospel warnings and the Gospel invitation without prejudice or discrimination of age, race or sex, then this little gem of Old Testament literature will have accomplished its purpose, and Jonah's near-death experience was not in vain.

---

[1] Luke 11:29. [2] Matt. 12:40. [3] 2 Kings 14:25. [4] Psalm 139:7, 8. [5] Luke 11:30. [6] Matt. 12:40. [7] See Acts 26:19, 20.

JONAH: STUDY GUIDE
For personal reflection and/or group discussion

1. It is sometimes said that Jonah is out of place among the prophets as there are no oracles in the book but a message of imminent judgement to one particular people. What do you think?

2. The notion of 'the repentance of God' may seem a tough one. Can you unpack it?
    How can it be explained in relation to Jonah's mission to Nineveh?

3. Do you feel that the way Jesus quoted the experience of Jonah — as a sign of His resurrection — confirms that the story of his incarceration in the great fish is literally true?

4. Is the real value and message of the Jonah story destroyed for those who regard it as mythical and allegorical?

5. What is the picture of God that emerges from Jonah?

6. Can it be true that God allows us to experience suffering and tribulation of any sort in order to call us back from our disobedience and prepare us to hear His voice 'the second time'?

MAJOR
Themes
from
MINOR
Prophets

Nahum

*The prophet
of God's
righteous
anger*

A WINDOW ON NAHUM'S TIME

'When angry, count to ten before you speak; if very angry, count to a hundred.' The wise advice of American president, Thomas Jefferson, came too late for Nahum! As we find him in Scripture, the prophet is very angry indeed! It is righteous anger, however, which, as we shall discover, is fully justified. It is anger which is vocal but not lethal, expressed in fiery words and terrifying eloquence. Nahum is reflecting the anger of a God of justice who is slow to pronounce judgement and swift to pardon the guilty who repent and amend their wicked ways.

The city of Nineveh was once more in the eye of the storm; the city where the reluctant Jonah had preached with dramatic effect a hundred years previously. The repentance of her citizens then would appear to have been shallow and super-ficial. The Assyrians reverted to their evil ways: unscrupulous trading, ruthless military might and relentless oppression. Nineveh was a 'bloody city'; a city of plunder. Its wicked ways were unceasing. God would use another nation as 'the rod of His anger', and Nineveh would be destroyed.

It is with relief that we discover that Nahum is not unaware of the other side of God's character. His wrath is 'the graver countenance of His love'; He is a refuge for those who trust Him. Nahum's rhetoric is like a mighty waterfall, across which a rainbow may be seen, the symbol of God's faithfulness and a reminder that our hopes for the future are founded on His grace.

Nahum is no narrow-minded patriot, but a man whose trust is in the God of history. Read his little book aloud, preferably with others, think of what the prophet might be saying to our world, but do not forget, in the end, to lift your eyes to the mountains to see the feet of Him who brings good news and proclaims peace. (Nahum 1:15.)

IT WAS THE Greek philosopher Aristotle who said, 'To be angry with the right person, at the right time, and with the right object, and in the right way is not easy and it is not everybody who can do it.' The prophet Nahum can!

When you open the pages of Nahum's unread book, you will be impressed by the power of his language, his rapid, excited style, oracles which are brilliantly written in colourful, graphic words.

We hear the cry of an outraged conscience. Nahum, poet and patriot, is a man with an acute sense of justice. Anger may only be one letter away from danger. But Nahum's anger is sanctified; it is the expression of God's holy, loving displeasure against sin.

Nahum is aware of a fundamental framework of morality in the world. He appreciates the beauty of righteousness, even as he abominates the brutality of evil. Judgement is a moral necessity, but his view of God's character is comprehensive and full orbed. His God is a God of dynamic justice and irresistible power, but He is also merciful, long-suffering and slow to anger; the Lord is good, a refuge in times of trouble. He cares for those who trust in Him.[1]

We know very little about the prophet Nahum. Elhosh, his home town, was probably in Judea. His name means comfort, compassion and consolation, which suggests that he is a sensitive, even an emotional man, who longs for God to vindicate His holiness and triumph over evil. The vision which inspired his prophecy came to him towards the end of the seventh century BC. He might even have found the temple in Jerusalem an appropriate setting, first to utter his prophecy and then to launch his book. Jeremiah might have been in the audience which was made up of people who were undoubtedly thrilled with the genius of his language, his grasp of history, his understanding of the politics of his day; but above all his knowledge of God's character. He would have been given a standing ovation and loud applause. It was a hopeful time in Jerusalem, because the young king, Josiah, had brought renewal to the land. The temple had been refurbished, the Book of the Law rediscovered and the passover celebrated with new power.[2] All idols were destroyed as the people repented and returned to the Lord. It was good news for Judah, but not for Nineveh, not for the mighty Assyrians.

We should pause and remind ourselves that Jonah had preached to Nineveh a hundred years before Nahum's time. Nineveh repented, but her repentance was short-lived. The Assyrian nation had reverted to a programme of endless cruelty, ruthless military might, unscrupulous commerce and unceasing evil. Nineveh was at that time the metropolis of the ancient world. The inner city was enclosed by a wall almost eight miles in its circumference. The River Tigris had been diverted to create a system of canals which made it in effect an island, and it was thought to be impregnable. It earned the infamous title of 'The Robber City'. Nahum's message is that Nineveh is doomed and will be destroyed, a catastrophe which he believed to be imminent: this proud city is to be annihilated, its splendid architecture and its treasures gone for ever. It is to become an empty void, a waste land — words which came to pass literally when the flooded city was overcome by the Babylonians and their allies in 612 BC.

Nahum describes the Lord as a 'jealous avenging God', puzzling words, until we understand what he means. God's jealousy is not of the green-eyed monster variety — vicious, selfish and abhorrent. It is 'a praiseworthy, virtuous quality which springs from a zeal to protect a love relationship and to avenge it when that relationship is broken'. The covenant theme, that of God's relationship with Israel, His chosen people, is threaded throughout these prophecies. Nahum is careful to draw a distinction between His indignation and fierce anger which none can understand, and His steadfast love for those who fulfil their vows of obedience to His commands.

Assyrian enemies have been lured to their fate as a man is seduced by a harlot and then devoured as if he has fallen into a den of lions. The awful lengths that man's cruelty can reach dry up all compassion for the wrongdoer in the self-satisfaction that God's justice will finally prevail. God says, "'I have no pleasure in the death of the wicked"'³ But even good men can be smug about God's judgements.

Nahum is so inspired as to describe how the great city of Nineveh will fall.⁴ She will brace herself for the onslaught and marshal all the strength of her armies in vain. Soldiers in scarlet uniforms will storm through the city streets; enemy chariots will dart about like lightning. The sluices will be opened to flood the city and the palaces will be destroyed. The treasures of silver and gold will be pillaged and plundered. Everyone will try to escape, but will stumble and fall in a state of shock. Imagine how Nahum's temple audience would cheer as they remembered stories of how the Assyrians had previously surrounded the city of Jerusalem in the reign of Hezekiah! They had sent the king messages of blasphemous contempt, boasting of their conquests and alleging that their God would not deliver them.⁵ It was at that time that Isaiah counselled the king and steadied the nerves of his people, so mocked and derided. "'He shall not come into this city,'" says the Lord, "I will defend this city and save it."' At that time, after a great slaughter, Sennacherib went home to Nineveh, only to be assassinated by his sons!

The cheering crowd provided Nahum with all the oxygen he needed to continue to pronounce his woes upon Nineveh. In quite terrifying language, which required no sound effects other than words, Nahum portrays the king of Assyria as fatally wounded. His onomatopoeia is tremendous: cracking whips, the clatter of wheels, galloping horses, jolting chariots! He sees the great city humiliated and in ruins, no better than the great Egyptian city of Thebes by the Nile which had been destroyed by the Assyrians at the height of their power. The prophet seems intoxicated by the exuberance of his eloquence and I can imagine his being lifted bodily, high above the adoring multitude, and carried from the temple precincts like a hero. He was surely the man of the hour!

As the tumult and the shouting die, and the prophet departs, we must be true to our mandate and ask some searching questions. Why is Nahum's message included in the canon of Scripture? It is not enough to admire his fiery rhetoric and triumphalism. We know that what he so vividly prophesied came to pass — that is a matter of history. But in what ways is God speaking to our world? What is of permanent value in the midst of his sound and fury?

First and foremost, we learn yet again that God is the God of history. We understand that if we would know that will of God for the world as well as for ourselves, we must know God's character — perfect love, perfect justice, great mercy and righteous anger. Kingdoms established upon cruelty and wickedness will ultimately perish; those who abuse power will, in the end, be destroyed by a power greater than themselves. As we look at our violent world, we may be inclined to ask, 'Is God still in control? Has His right hand lost its grasp?' The Bible encourages us to rejoice and celebrate the glorious certainty that ultimately all evil will be destroyed; the day of the Lord will surely come. It is a fearful thing to fall into the hands of the living God.[6]

Violence is not the way to achieve justice; it is self-defeating. We need to look no further than Northern Ireland, or South Africa, or the nation groups of former Yugoslavia. Violence intensified and prolonged the bitterness, pushing back the cause of durable peace. The assassination of Yitzhak Rabin shocked and stunned the whole world. The untimely death of this 'valiant and courageous champion of peace' as Dr Billy Graham, a life-long friend, described him, did nothing to further the peace process in Israel. It only served to fan the flames of hatred and division. *Shalom*, the peace that passes understanding, God's peace, the only desirable end, is never served by violent means.

I must bring back Nahum for a final word, not now in anger, but, true to the meaning of his name, as a comforter. These are times when our hearts melt with fear, and our knees tremble. We, too, may be enveloped in the darkness of our circumstances. It may be the tragedy of a still-born child, all the hopes and expectations during the months of pregnancy dashed in disappointment and despair. It may be in a lingering illness in old age with the loss of faculties and independence, when the sufferer longs for the sweet release of death. It is with a quieter voice that Nahum repeats his comforting words: 'He cares in times of trouble for those who trust in Him.' It is an amazing thing that the God who controls the universe loves those who keep His vows and celebrate the festivals of salvation. With a final dramatic word of farewell, Nahum lifts his eyes to the hills. 'Look,' he cries, 'there on the mountains, the feet of one who brings good news, who proclaims peace, news of happiness.' Do I hear you burst spontaneously into song? . . .

> 'Our God reigns, our God reigns!
> Ends of the earth, see the salvation of your God,
> Jesus is Lord, is Lord,
> Before the nations, He has bared His holy arm:
> Our God reigns, our God reigns.'
> *(Words by Leonard Smith Jun., based on Isa. 52:7, 10, and Nahum 1:15.)*

---

[1] Nahum 1:2-8. [2] 2 Kings 22 and 23. [3] Ezek. 33:11. [4] Nahum 4. [5] Isa. 36:18-20; 37:10-13, 36-38. [6] Heb. 10:31.

NAHUM: STUDY GUIDE

For personal reflection and/or group discussion

1. 'A jealous God', seems to us, in this and other contexts, to be a rather unwelcome and inappropriate description of God. See also the second commandment (Exodus 20:5). What do you think it means?

2. What sort of circumstances and situations make you angry — and not only in your own personal situation, but in society and indeed the world?

3. 'Go ahead and be angry. You do well to be angry — but don't use your anger as a fuel for revenge. And don't stay angry. Don't go to bed angry. Don't give the devil that kind of foothold in your life.' (Paul's words in Ephesians 4:26 as translated in *The Message*, the New Testament in contemporary English by Eugene H. Peterson.)
    Do you agree that Paul's words (quoting Psalm 4:4) are wise and acceptable?
    If so, why?

4. 'There is an anger without which the world would be a poorer place.' (William Barclay.) Can you think of people in recent history who had 'the right kind of anger'?
    When was our Lord Jesus angry?

5. When is anger sinful?

MAJOR
Themes
from
MINOR
Prophets

Habakkuk

The perplexed prophet

A WINDOW ON HABAKKUK'S TIME

Before we meet our next guest, Habakkuk, on our walk through the minor prophets, we need to prepare for a perplexing experience. We may look with confidence to the Apostle Paul who, in his superb and beautiful hymn of love in his first letter to Corinth, writes about the incompleteness of our knowledge and understanding concerning the mystery of faith.

'We see in a mirror dimly, but then face to face. Now I know in part; then I shall understand fully.' (1 Cor. 13:12, RSV.) It is the 'now' and the 'then' that are crucial, for the prophet and for ourselves. We may not understand in the 'now' how God is working His purpose out, but having acknowledged this, there is the assurance that all will become clear. The mist will lift as the weather improves and the sun will shine brightly once more.

The genius of Habakkuk, however, is to reveal that even in our perplexity, we are not left to shiver in apprehension and fear. 'The just shall live by faith,' he declares in a formula that fashions the theology of salvation and formed the watchword of the Reformation.

Habakkuk tells us very little about himself, but we can identify with him as we look at our violent world. Why is God so patient, so tolerant, so silent? Why does a righteous, loving God not intervene? Why does God allow this or that to happen? The 'why' will turn into 'wait', the protests will become a psalm, the murmuring will turn into music. The prophet called up the choirmaster and the orchestra and they celebrated the splendour, the power and the sovereignty of God. In the strength of the Lord, surefooted once more, he leaves behind him the valley of doubt and disbelief for the uplands of faith, hope and love. We may do the same!

MANY PEOPLE remember that fateful night when the Pan Am clipper *Maid of the Seas* exploded over the small Scottish town of Lockerbie. It was an act of human wickedness which shocked the world. Some asked the question: 'Why should a God of love allow such an atrocity, in which so many innocent people perished and so many more were bereaved? Where was God when it happened? Absent? Looking the other way?'

'Our first act of pained, protesting faith is to turn to God in reproach, even in anger.' Those were the words of a leading clergyman at a memorial service shortly after the disaster.

The question 'Why?' is frequently on our lips, in suffering or bereavement, when natural disasters occur, when we contemplate our violent world. Why is God silent? Why does He not intervene, this God of infinite love and power?

I cannot wait to introduce you to Habakkuk, for in his slender prophecy he wrestles with this problem, and like Job dares to argue with God. His book reads like the script of a play, a dialogue with God, a question-and-answer session (chapters 1 and 2). Read it aloud with a partner and play some instrumental music as a background. Habakkuk would like that; and especially when you read the beautiful and brilliant psalm at the end (chapter 3).

The prophet lived some 600 years before Christ. The people of the Northern Kingdom of Israel were long since lost in exile. The power of Assyria, like that of Egypt, had been eclipsed by the Chaldeans from Babylon, whose armies would advance like a desert wind to overcome Judah and capture the city of Jerusalem. Habakkuk might have been a Levite, a singer in the temple choir, or perhaps an instrumentalist, dedicating his oracle to the director of music and the leader of the orchestra. His name is said to mean 'a plant that clings', which seems strangely appropriate as his story unfolds. Like Jacob he wrestles with God and cries out, 'I will not let you go unless you bless me!'[1]

As he looks at the world of violence and injustice, strife and conflict, the law paralysed, the prophet's impatience boils over.

He finds God's delays hard to live with. Why does God not act? Why does He tolerate such wickedness? 'Why are you not listening? Why do you not intervene to rescue the righteous and punish the evildoers?'[2] We empathize with his anguish and his passion for righteousness. God's answer seems only to deepen his distress and increase his perplexity. It is revealed that God will punish Judah for their evil ways by using the all-conquering Babylonians. Their spectacular cavalry and unstoppable foot soldiers will invade the land and Jerusalem will be destroyed. The prophet is outraged at the very thought — the Sovereign Lord, whose eyes are too pure even to look on evil, appointing such a nation as Babylon to discipline His people! How can He do such a thing? How can God use such treacherous people to bring judgement on a chosen race who, for all their shortcomings, are not as evil as they are?[3]

Habakkuk brings his indignation under control. He so wisely ascends a watch tower, above the turmoil of his tempestuous world, and waits to see how events will unfold; and with a quieter heart, perhaps, to hear how the Lord will answer. How like the Psalmist he is when he writes, 'When I thought how to understand this, it seemed to me a wearisome task, until I went into the sanctuary of God; then I perceived their end.'[4]

In the midst of the mysteries of circumstance and our struggle to understand the meaning of events, unbroken fellowship with God must be maintained. We live in a small slice of time and God lives in eternity. We cannot see beyond the horizon, however high the watch-tower may be. God is working His purpose out. The Babylonians will not escape God's wrath. In their pride, they, too, will eventually be overthrown. Meanwhile, the prophet is reminded that 'the righteous live by faith', great words woven into the theology of salvation by the Apostle Paul, words which became the watchword in the Reformation and are associated so memorably with Martin Luther.

We soon begin to realize that as his angry speculation

about what God seems to be doing and not doing in the world subsides, Habakkuk's trust in God's providence and power begins to flourish again. Israel's hope is in the Lord for evermore. The prophet turns his wrath and indignation away from God and taunts the Chaldeans[5] in words that vividly describe their evil ways and which predict the inevitable judgement that will come upon them. The mood changes as he utters 'Woes' against the aggressors who, in their greed, plunder the resources of other nations, ruin other peoples' lives, and expand their empires by violence and bloodshed. He continues his 'Woes' against man's inhumanity to man, against those who shamelessly treat fellow human beings with contempt, challenges the futility of idol worship, of lifeless stones covered in gold and silver but without breath! He mocks them as they try in vain to wake them up and give them guidance, but his mockery melts into majesty as he lifts up his voice in a glorious crescendo of sound, 'The Lord is in His Holy Temple; let all the earth be silent before Him.' He has already declared his faith in another grand chorus: 'The earth will be filled with the knowledge of the glory of the Lord as the waters cover the sea.'

However, the best is still to come (chapter 3), the crown of his whole composition, a final movement as great as any in Hebrew literature. It is a result of his very real fellowship with God who understands his perplexity, and is patient in his questioning, and who reveals more of Himself, of His majesty and power. Habakkuk bows in awe before the Almighty; he recites again His mighty deeds, this God who 'shook the earth and made the nations tremble', this God whose ways are eternal, splendid like the sunrise. He is the God of the Exodus, the great deliverer.

As the torrent of language comes to an end, celebrating the omnipotence of God, his heart is hushed before the Lord. Look back to the point where this final psalm begins and hear the prophet pray, 'Lord, revive your work in the midst of the years', as if to say to God, 'Now do again in our time the great deeds you used to do.' Inner distress gives way to quiet confidence, and speculative doubt to triumphant faith. Now that he is ready to wait patiently for God to act, the end is not in doubt: the victory of righteousness and the defeat of evil.

It is obvious that Habakkuk is a musician, for his conclusion is rather like Handel's *Messiah*, as he sings, 'I will greatly rejoice in the Lord; my soul shall be joyful in God my Saviour.' There is, however, a most revealing postscript and it is added because the prophet may suspect that we have discovered the meaning of his name, a 'plant that clings', in which there is more than a hint of feebleness and dependency.

'The Sovereign Lord is my strength; he makes my feet like the feet of a deer, he enables me to go on to the heights.' He who clings in the beginning, climbs in the end! He is light-hearted, and sure-footed, undaunted by the most difficult high places in his path of life.

In our experience we, too, must dare to trust in God, as someone has written; 'No paralysing panic, no irresponsible escapism, no morbid pessimism — but firm faith should characterize God's people.'

The greatest hymn that was ever written on Divine providence was by one who closely resembles our prophet Habakkuk, William Cowper, a brilliant and versatile man who suffered periods of deep depression throughout his life. It is said that Cowper was on the verge of suicide when he wrote those memorable lines, 'God moves in a mysterious way'. When the hymn was published in 1773, it was entitled 'Light shineth out of darkness' — it was the spontaneous overflow of powerful feeling — an apt description of the prophecy itself as well as the hymn. The verses are a beautiful commentary on this remarkable book. The last verse was inspired by the words of Jesus as He prepared to wash the feet of Simon Peter in the Upper Room of the Last Supper. 'What I am doing you do not know now, but afterwards you will understand.'[6]

'Blind unbelief is sure to err,
And scan His work in vain;
God is His own interpreter,
And He will make it plain.'

Someone promised C. H. Spurgeon when he was only 10
years old that he would have sixpence if he learnt the hymn by
heart and if he promised to use it if he became a preacher! If
only we could so applaud Habakkuk for his book, so loudly and
persistently, as to bring him back on to the stage and sing
Cowper's hymn as an encore!

Now that we have cut open the pages of yet another of these
obscure and unread books, we can surely see how relevant are
the prophet's words for our world, for our own experience.
How many of us have turned to God in an act of 'pained, protesting faith' like the people of Lockerbie. We have watched a
loved one struggle in vain to survive a serious illness; we hear
the news — a recital of catastrophe here, calamity there. We
have cried out in despair, 'Why, Lord? Why me? Why were You
so deaf to my prayers?' In our fearfulness we discover that the
dreaded clouds are big with mercy; the bitter taste of the bud
becomes the sweetness of the flower. In the midst of evil we
find goodness; in the midst of darkness we find light. Our lives
are touched by the God of all comfort, the God of hope.

---

[1] Gen. 32:24-27. [2] See Hab. 1:1-4. [3] Hab. 1:5-17. [4] Ps. 73:16, 17. [5] Hab. 2:6-20.
[6] John 13:7.

HABAKKUK: STUDY GUIDE

For personal reflection and/or group discussion

1. 'If God is all-powerful and all-loving, why does He not intervene in our world?'
    How do we respond to this question?*

2. 'So often the innocent suffer, the guilty go free.' People often say something like this, raising the age-old problem of God's justice.
    How do you react to remarks like that?

3. In pastoral counselling a frequent problem is that of unanswered prayer and the frustration that is experienced when God is (or seems to be) silent.
    How does Habakkuk's message help us in that kind of situation?

4. It is fair to assume that Habakkuk was a musician. How can music help us in times of anxiety?

5. 'The Book of Psalms contains the whole music of the heart of man, the lyrical burst of his tenderness, the moan of his penitence, the pathos of his sorrow, the triumph of his victory, the despair of his defeat, the firmness of his confidence, the rapture of his assured hope.' (from *The Psalms in Human Life* by R. W. Pothero.)
    Try to recall the times in your experience when the Psalms have helped you. It would be helpful to share your story to encourage others.

* If you are having serious problems with this question, buy a copy of *Is God Still in the Healing Business?* by David Marshall (published by Autumn House). It was written to help answer it.

MAJOR
Themes
from
MINOR
Prophets

Zephaniah

*The prophet of
imminent gloom
and ultimate
glory*

A WINDOW ON ZEPHANIAH'S TIME

Before I invite you to meet Zephaniah and read his prophecy, I want you to imagine that you are enjoying a walk with friends in the mountains, anywhere in the world. It is a lovely day when you set out. I will take it for granted that you are well equipped for any emergency. A happy, invigorating and challenging day is in prospect.

Quite suddenly, however, storm clouds sweep across the sky. You hear the distant thunder and see a flash of lightning. The rain begins to fall in torrents, but you find shelter in a mountain hut. Here you have a grandstand view of the spectacular storm. Loud thunder claps reverberate over the mountain peaks, the lightning flashes and forks to illuminate, momentarily, the valleys. It is an awesome experience. You console yourselves with your flask of hot drink and your chocolate. However, the sky begins to clear, the thunder and lightning are no more, the rains cease and you are in bright sunshine once again!

That is the sort of experience which awaits you with Zephaniah. You walk straight into the thunderstorm of God's righteous anger and judgement, the day of divine wrath. You must make allowances for Zephaniah, however. He is a young man of royal pedigree. His indignation is because, in the last fifty years, the reforms of good King Hezekiah, from whom he is descended, have been reversed as God's people have followed pagan and idolatrous priests and have forsaken their covenant with God. Judgement is inevitable, and not only for Judah, but on the surrounding nations. Jerusalem will surely fall to an invading army, and many will go into exile; but disaster is not the end of the story. The thunderstorm of God's judgement will pass as, once more, the sun breaks through, the brilliant sunshine of divine blessing and 'the coming of the glad day when God's people will become a praise among all the peoples of the earth'. Enjoy your adventure and savour the lovely promise with which the prophecy ends: 'I will bring you home.'

SOME YEARS AGO a distinguished member of the House of Lords rose to speak on the ills of modern society, on crime, violence and lawlessness. In a passage which surprised many in the Upper House that day, the noble lord went on to say:

'May I suggest we might reintroduce conscience and reintroduce the devil?' With perhaps a glance at the Bishops of the Church of England who also sit with the peers of the realm, he added, 'And, dare I say it, the answer lies in the churches.'

His lordship's words ring true for our world now; we need to recognize the fearful reality of satanic evil and refuse to extenuate, excuse and apologize for wrongdoing with a host of psychological and sociological excuses. Sin is not a novelty in society, even if modern technology and the media only serve to multiply and magnify evil deeds, but the consequence for individuals and nations need to be proclaimed. God is unchanging in His holiness, in His grief and anger, in His righteous judgements, but, above all, in His steadfast love for all the human race. The ultimate victory of righteousness is never in doubt, and neither is the task of the churches!

The prophet Zephaniah would have been at home in the House of Lords, for he was of royal ancestry. He was the great-great-grandson of the good King Hezekiah. He was familiar with court circles, and, as a resident in Jerusalem, he knew the city well. He was almost certainly a very young man, perhaps no more than 20 years old, when he began to prophesy with all the vigour, indignation and zeal of youth. We may deduce from other historical data that he grew up in the reign of Manasseh, a notoriously wicked king, who 'shed very much innocent blood, till he had filled Jerusalem from one end to another'.[1] Those infamous years were known as 'the killing time', when the evil king led the people astray and committed detestable things, undoing all the reforms of King Hezekiah who trusted the Lord like no other kings before or after him. What a heartbreak for the young prophet to see all the sound policies of his great ancestor reversed, to see Judah become a living contradiction of all that was enshrined in her covenant relationship with God, to see her engaging in idol worship, spiritism and the occult.

Come with me to meet this splendid young man, because to see him is to admire him and to discover that he is a man of many gifts. He is eloquent and compelling, but never arrogant or rude. We shall be impressed with his humility, a quality of character which in his impassioned speeches he urges on others. He will, no doubt, tell us of his high regard for Isaiah and almost certainly acknowledge his indebtedness to Jeremiah who might have recognized him as 'the man of the hour' and helped to prepare him for a prophetic role at a time of crisis. The name Zephaniah means, 'God has guarded or hidden'. Some have thought that at his birth he might have been hidden, as Moses was, and so saved from slaughter for some great purpose. There is an echo of such an experience when he urges the people to seek the Lord. 'Seek righteousness, seek humility,' he cries, and adds these words, 'perhaps you may be hidden in the day of the Lord's anger.'[2]

It was crisis time in Jerusalem when King Amon, a young man of only 22 years, succeeded King Manasseh, who had reigned for fifty-five terrible years, and King Amon behaved just as his evil father had done, forsaking the Lord and worshipping idols. After only two years, Amon was assassinated by a conspiracy of palace officials and an 8-year-old boy, Josiah, became king. There was then no hiding place for Zephaniah! The nation had to be warned of the awful consequences of its recent history; but in the vacuum that had been created, a minor inheriting the throne, there was another urgent task, namely this, that Josiah had to be protected from the evil influence of wicked men, and educated to walk in the paths of righteousness, to worship the Lord, do what was right in His eyes and follow the example of his ancestor, David. Then there had to be a clarion call for the nation to repent, for the revocation of all idols and their destruction, and a reformation in worship and government.

There is little doubt the young prophet, Zephaniah, was a confidant of the young King in those formative years, so that when he became of age Josiah was fired with a zeal for revival which defied his youth and inexperience. It will help us to read Zephaniah's prophecy, if we remember that even as he vents his anger on all who had turned their backs upon the Lord and all who had indulged in violence and fraud, he sees beyond the day of judgement; and in the dark sky and among the threatening clouds he sees 'the rainbow of God's love arching the horizon of the future'. His prophecy is indeed one of judgement, but also an apocalypse of ultimate glory.

Let us imagine that we have slipped into a public meeting in Jerusalem where Zephaniah is billed to speak. There is a buzz of excited conversation as we take our seats and an air of great expectation. The audience is hushed as the platform party take their places. The chairman has some kind and complimentary words about the young prophet, who comes with a reputation for outspokenness, integrity and charisma. But who is prepared for the message he is about to deliver?

'What I have to say,' he begins, 'is none other than the message I have received from the Lord. The Lord says, "I will sweep away everything from the face of the earth . . . I will sweep away . . . I will sweep away . . . I will stretch out My hand against Judah and against all who live in Jerusalem."'

The audience is stunned by the rhetoric, scarcely comprehending the gravity of his words. There is condemnation of idolatry, of the worship of false gods, of the occult. Those who have become rich by deceit and exploitation of the poor are condemned. 'I will punish . . . .' The ominous words are repeated as Zephaniah describes how the Lord will search out those who are self satisfied and indifferent — they are in for a rude awakening — and he vividly describes what the great day of the Lord will mean. He seems almost to over-reach himself as he proclaims how the divine wrath will consume the whole world!

We are uneasy and are about to leave because we can bear to hear no more of such days of darkness and distress, when suddenly, with a dramatic change of tone, the preacher lowers his voice and speaks with earnestness and compassion.

'Pull yourselves together,' he urges. 'Come to your senses; seek the Lord; obey His commandments; humble yourselves before the Lord. There may yet be a way of escape. God may yet relent so that judgement may be averted; God can change His mind.'

I imagine an interval here while the speaker recovers from his *tour de force* and refreshes himself. They are all eager to hear what else he has to say and soon settle in their places. At first, however, they are dismayed and disappointed until they realize that he has turned his fiery eloquence on other nations and then they feel more comfortable. Zephaniah preaches against the Philistines who live by the sea, whose pastures will be returned to the house of Judah. There is rapturous applause which is repeated as others are also condemned: Moab and Ammon who will become like Sodom and Gomorrah because they have insulted the people of the Lord; Assyria will also be destroyed; and the proud city of Nineveh, so self-confident and secure, will be a ruin, utterly desolate and dry as a desert. The audience are already on their feet, not realizing that the message for their neighbours is also a message for them, the people of Jerusalem.

There is, I imagine, another interval. People can only stand so much, and as you read you may feel like giving up. 'I can take no more,' I hear you say. 'Enough is enough!' But wait; the best is yet to be. The city of Jerusalem and all the people who dwell there have indeed rebelled against the Lord and have been disobedient. Politicians, prophets, priests are all guilty, but . . . and here Zephaniah lifts his eyes heavenward and opens his arms as if to embrace his eager audience:

'The Lord is still here in the midst of turmoil and chaos. He is altogether righteous; morning by morning He brings justice to His people. He does not fail.'

The prophecy ends with a song of joy. Those whose trust is in the Lord, who can call on His name and stand shoulder to shoulder to serve Him in obedience, have nothing to fear. In this final passage of rare beauty, Zephaniah excels himself as

He draws wonderful images of the Lord. He is the King who is in the midst, who promises security. He is the warrior who gives victory, and He is the bridegroom who will take delight in the meek and humble. 'He will quiet you with His love and rejoice over you with singing.' In words of ecstasy, as if the bridegroom carries His loved one over the threshold, he adds these words: ' . . . at that time, I will bring you home.'

As is usual with words of prophecy, they often have an imminent as well as an ultimate meaning. Zephaniah's campaign for reform inspired the young King Josiah to act. He began by repairing and renovating the Temple, using an utterly trustworthy work force. The Book of the Law, undoubtedly the Book of Deuteronomy, was rediscovered in the process and read in public with dramatic effect. Idols were destroyed; the covenant was renewed 'in the presence of the Lord', and the Passover was celebrated with more sincerity and rejoicing than there had been for centuries. History reveals, however, that the reformation did not last. The judgements were fulfilled when Jerusalem fell to the Babylonians and many of the people were taken into exile.

The ultimate fulfilment of Zephaniah's prophecies are yet to be, when that great day of the Lord comes in the return of Christ and the glorious Kingdom of God. But meanwhile, what has the prophet to say to us and to our world, to the Church and the new people of God? Paul's words to Timothy spring to mind: 'Let no man despise your youth, but set the believers an example in speech and conduct, in love, in faith, in purity.'[3] What the young lack in experience they more than compensate for in the freshness of their enthusiasm and their boundless energy. We need to recognize those who are gifted as our prophet was, and use them in the Church's mission to the world.

Sometimes, in our personal lives, our circumstances and adversities seem as chastisement; not joyous, but grievous; but again, in words of Scripture, 'nevertheless, afterwards, they yield the peaceable fruits of righteousness.'

By now, the wheel has come full circle and the noble lord we mentioned at the beginning speaks again. 'Whatever happened to conscience?' he asks again. 'Why is the Church failing to speak out in times like these, challenging the godlessness of the present time and calling on our people, not only to recognize the power of evil, but in repentance and faith, to rediscover Jesus and how lives can be transformed when we turn to Him?' It was a canon of St Paul's Cathedral who had a great concern for the social application of the Christian faith, and who wrote words which Zephaniah would have loved to sing:

> 'Judge Eternal, throned in splendour,
> Lord of hosts and King of kings,
> With thy living fire of judgement
> Purge this realm of bitter things.
> Solace all its wide dominions
> With the healing of Thy wings.'

---

[1] 2 Kings 21:16. [2] Zeph. 2:3. [3] 1 Tim. 4:12.

ZEPHANIAH: STUDY GUIDE

For personal reflection and/or group discussion

1. 'In this liberal age, we tend naturally to avoid any thought of God's judgement.' (David Watson.)
   How far do you think these words are true?

2. Angry young men and women are to be found in all parts of our world. Should we praise their youthful courage — or restrain them?
   What are the issues which concern them most?

3. To say that 'history is bunk' and teaches us nothing is manifestly untrue. What can we learn from the experience of Zephaniah and his times?

4. You were 'invited' to a public meeting where Zephaniah was speaking. Did you:
   a) feel like leaving the meeting before it finished?
   b) join in the applause?
   c) want to ask a question and if so what would you have asked?

5. Do you think the 'Church' *is* failing to speak out in times like these? What should the Church be saying?

MAJOR
Themes
from
MINOR
Prophets

Obadiah

The roots of bitterness and the fruits of repentance

A WINDOW ON OBADIAH'S TIME

Karl Barth, the world-famous Swiss theologian, recommended preachers to have the Bible in one hand and the newspaper in the other. He believed that the Christian proclamation must be tested by Scripture, but also that it should be made relevant to the contemporary scene. In short, the message should be both biblical and topical; it should reveal both the grace and judgement of God with the understanding that God's judgement is the flipside of His grace.

Reach, then, for a serious newspaper. You might read there about the hatred between Jews and Palestinians, engaging in a stuttering peace process, or the residual hatred and bitterness in Ireland. The world may be different where you live as situations change and solutions evolve, but the problems will be substantially the same.

As you put the paper down, don't reach for the Bible for a moment! The little book of Obadiah is an uninviting and unpromising read unless you see first parallels in our time. It is a story of enmity and hatred, a cry for vengeance, a prophecy of judgement. The historical background is as fascinating as it is frightening and frustrating. The animosity between Edom and Israel is traced back to its source, but there is a deep-seated conviction that God holds the reins of history. We may recoil from what appears to be gloating over the disasters suffered by others; but emerging from these least-popular words of Scripture is a very personal message. Hate is a festering sore, mutual hatred will take us nowhere; bitter memories must be healed, reconciliation is far more important than recrimination and retribution. This obscure prophet, Obadiah, has a flair for fiery speech, but amid the sound and fury, he shares the secret of his confidence that in the end the Kingdom will be the Lord's.

'OBADIAH IS THE shortest book of all the books of the Old Testament, and yet it is not to be passed by, for this penny has Caesar's image and superscription upon it; it is stamped with divine authority.'

So wrote Matthew Henry in his commentary on this obscure fragment of the Bible.

As we open up the page, we may well wonder what is the significance of its insignificance! What is its relevance to our world? What, if any, is its message for us? The prophet writes what he sees — it is the *vision* of Obadiah — and he records what God has spoken.

It was obviously an important message at the time, and if we persevere we shall discover that there is a message for us today.

The challenge and fascination of Obadiah is that to understand it we need to have an acquaintance with Scriptures from Genesis to the Letter to the Hebrews! When we have grasped the historical background, we shall see emerging a very profound and spiritual lesson, namely this; that roots of bitterness produce fruits of self-destruction. We shall learn that untreated wounds poison not only those afflicted by them, but also infect our relationships with others. The healing of memories is a therapy that is as important now as at any other time.

We know very little of Obadiah's personal history. His is a very common name, but it has an interesting meaning: 'the servant of the Lord.' As his name is, so is he! Twenty-five years after Nineveh was overcome by the Babylonians, as Nahum had predicted, Jerusalem was conquered by the same all-powerful enemy (c 587BC). It was about that time that Obadiah prophesied. The message God gave him was for Edom, the kingdom adjoining Israel and south of the Dead Sea, also known as Seir or Mount Seir. It was an infertile region, mountainous and thought to be impregnable. Teman, Bozrah and Sela — now referred to as Petra — were Edomite towns. Petra was a spectacular rocky fortress, still a great attraction for horse-riding tourists today.

Edom (which means 'Red') was the nickname for Esau, with

whom our story begins; the Edomites were descendants of
Abraham. There was a situation of perpetual hostility and
enmity between the house of Esau and the house of Jacob, an
ever-increasing hatred as the centuries passed. How did it all
start and why were the Edomites the sworn enemy of Israel?

Astonishingly, the enmity began in the womb! — yes, with
Rebekah, the wife of Isaac. The woman was unable to have
children, a disappointing condition that can cause heartbreak
and frustration. However, Isaac prayed to the Lord and in
answer to his prayer Rebekah conceived. The pregnancy was a
difficult one. The mother-to-be suffered such discomfort and
distress that she challenged God in her prayers. '"Why is this
happening to me?"' she complained. Then it was revealed that
she was carrying twin boys, struggling and in conflict before
they were born! '"Two nations are in your womb,"' said God.
'"Two peoples shall be divided; the one shall be stronger than
the other and the elder will serve the younger."'[1] The ancient
writer vividly describes the circumstance of the births. The
first child was red and the little infant was like a hairy garment.
As his brother was born, his hand was grasping the other
baby's head. As the boys grew up their characters were completely different. Esau was aggressive and vigorously active as a
man of the earth, sensuous, materialistic, locked in time and
unaware of eternity. Jacob was quieter, more devious and, inter-
mittently, more spiritual. The rivalry between them was only
aggravated and indeed fostered by their unwise parents, the
father showing favour to Esau and Rebekah to Jacob.

The story as it continues is stranger than fiction. Esau
sold his birthright for a pottage of red lentils, in a rash moment
when he came home from the open country famished for want
of food. We know the feeling, if not the folly! There is yet more
drama; as the story is told in great detail by the ancient story-
teller. Isaac was then old and unable to see. It was not difficult
to deceive him into bestowing his blessing, which was designed
for Esau, upon Jacob. It was a mother's intrigue and her son's
cunning. The classic story is one you really will enjoy as you

read it for yourself, since to attempt to tell it in other words is only to mutilate it.[2]

We can begin to imagine the grudges and the furious anger of Esau against his brother Jacob, and his thirst for revenge. Strong man as he was, Esau wept as he realized he had been deceived and cheated twice by a brother, true to his name — meaning a deceiver. He resolved to kill him; it was to be his only consolation. It was the intervention of Rebekah who, sensing the danger Jacob was in, urged him to flee to his uncle, Laban, until the fury subsided. Esau and his family moved to the hill country of Seir where his descendants remained, still perpetuating, generation after generation, the hatred and enmity which we have described. 'Hatred is too great a burden to bear,' said that great fighter for freedom, Martin Luther King. It always seems to justify itself, but instead of vindication it only breeds defeat and despair.

At the time of the Exodus, Moses pleaded to be allowed safe passage along the King's Highway on the Israelites' journey from Egypt, with all its hardships and ill-treatment, to Canaan; but in spite of assurances that the Israelites would behave impeccably, even promising they would pay for food and water, permission was refused. '"You shall not pass through,"' and a large and powerful army came out against them to prevent it.[3] The house of Jacob had always desired and actively sought reconciliation with the house of Esau, only to be rebuffed.

The sorry story which is behind this strange oracle of Obadiah is not yet over. At the time of the fall of Jerusalem to the Babylonians, not only did the Edomites refuse to come to Israel's aid; but they gave every assistance to the invading army. When the exiles in Babylon sat down by the river and wept, they remembered Edom's treachery.

'Remember, O Lord, what the Edomites did on the day Jerusalem fell. "Tear it down," they cried, "tear it down to its foundations!"'[4]

The prophet Jeremiah had prophesied the doom and destruction of Edom in words vivid with terror and divine punishment.[5] This was surely 'the message from the Lord' to which Obadiah refers as he begins his prophecy.

It has been a long, historical journey, and we must pause for rest and refreshment. We shall find it in the verse which is the key to unlock the door of our understanding and allow us to enter the meaning of the Scripture: '"As you have done, it shall be done to you."'[6] In His great sermon Jesus expressed the reverse truth in His much-quoted and memorable words, '"In everything, do to others what you would have them do to you, for this sums up the Law and the Prophets."'[7]

Obadiah now proclaims the fate of Edom as he calls upon other nations to rise up and do battle against her. '"I will make you small . . . you will be utterly despised . . . disaster awaits you."' His words are like thunder, reverberating across the dark sky with flashes of lightning, as with vigorous eloquence and poetic language he continues, '"Though you soar aloft like the eagle and make your nest among the stars, I will bring you down,"' declares the Lord. Edom's pride in their homes in the heights among the clefts of the rocks will be shattered because of the violence done to Jacob. The prophet recounts what they did 'in the day when Jerusalem was overthrown', their unforgivable behaviour. They gloated over Israel's defeat and rejoiced in the ruin of the city; they looted and pillaged and even prevented those who tried to escape. Their evil deeds would return on their own heads! The destruction of Edom came to pass, little remaining in that inhospitable region save that remarkable and unique antiquity we know as Petra.

It will not surprise us that when the prophet Obadiah turns his focus upon Israel, he speaks of hope and restoration, of deliverance and repossession. It is poetic justice upon Edom, but for the covenant people of God the future is bright with God's promises. 'The kingdom will be the Lord's' is the confident clarion call with which the prophecy ends.

At last, our patience is to have its own reward as we ask

what is the message which Obadiah has for us today which justifies his place in Holy Scripture. There are important principles, foremost of which is this: God's righteousness cannot forever be flouted by godless people. God holds the reins of history in His hands. We learn also that those who persecute the people of God will receive divine retribution. As another of the prophets put it, 'He who touches you, touches the apple of His eye.' We see clearly that those roots of bitterness, 'bitter noxious weeds', must be eradicated from the hearts and minds of individuals as well as communities and nations — in families, in churches, in society — otherwise, they go on to contaminate the whole of life. There is another warning here. We must guard against being profane — absorbing the material and despising the spiritual, living in time and neglecting eternity, thinking exclusively of what is imminent and ignoring the transcendent. It is now that, having begun our study-trail in Genesis, we end in that most Jewish of New Testament letters, the Hebrews, where the writer sums up the message of Obadiah in a masterly fashion:

'Make every effort to live in peace with all men and be holy; without holiness no one will see the Lord.'

'Holiness,' wrote Bishop Westcott, 'is the preparation for the presence of God.'

The writer to the Hebrews continues, 'See that no one misses the grace of God and that no bitter root grows up to cause trouble!' Then there flashes upon his inward eye the vision of Esau! 'See that no one is profane (AV), immoral, like Esau, who for a single meal sold his inheritance rights and afterwards could bring about no change of mind, though he sought the blessing with tears.'[8] In searching for a prayer with which to conclude, I remember these words:

'Come, Holy Spirit, to cleanse and renew us:
Purge us from evil and fill us with power.
Thus shall the waters of healing flow through us;

So shall revival be born in this hour.

Let us then ruthlessly cast out those roots of bitterness and carefully cultivate the fruits of the spirit.'

---

[1] Gen. 25:19ff. [2] Gen. 27. [3] Num. 20:14-21. [4] Ps. 137. [5] Jer. 49:7-22. [6] Obad. 15. [7] Matt. 7:12. [8] Heb. 12:14-17.

OBADIAH: STUDY GUIDE

For personal reflection and/or group discussion

1. 'As you have done it, it shall be done to you,' wrote Obadiah.
   'Do to others what you would have them do to you,' said Jesus.
   Why is the positive note in the way Jesus states 'the Golden Rule'
   much to be preferred?

2. 'There is a time to love and a time to hate.' (Eccles. 3:8.)
   Can you comment on this quotation from what many think of as a
   rather splendid poem, a famous passage of Scripture?

3. Some well-chosen words of Martin Luther King are quoted in the text:
   'Hate is too great a burden to bear.'
   Discuss those things in American society which Martin Luther King
   hated and the non-violent ways in which he worked to bring about
   changes and, indeed, for which he gave his life.
   Do you 'have a dream' for the world to compare with his?

4. When hasty words cannot be recalled and hasty actions cannot be
   undone, what options are open to us?
   Is there a way open for 'second thoughts'?

5. The healing of memories is a therapy much discussed nowadays.
   How far can this therapy improve the happiness of individuals who
   are suffering from bad memories?
   Are there dangers in such counselling?
   Especially, perhaps, with children?

MAJOR
Themes
from
MINOR
Prophets

Haggai

*The prophet of
priorities and
encouragement*

A WINDOW ON HAGGAI'S TIME

No prophet of the Old Testament would be more welcome in our day than the man we are about to meet, Haggai. His brief book is one of the jewels of Scripture. He is the optimist who sees an opportunity in every difficulty; as opposed to the pessimist who sees a difficulty in every opportunity. If you found the doom and gloom of his predecessors monotonous, you will delight in Haggai's positive thinking, vigorous enthusiasm, and in his forthright and uncompromising messages.

The people of God had returned to their homeland after the Babylonian captivity. It was the period of Israel's rebirth. However, although they had made a fine start on rebuilding their city, more especially the ruined temple of Solomon, they had lost heart. The work had ceased and, concurrently, their economy gone into recession and inflation was rampant. People were wrapped up in self-interest; their priorities were all wrong. Apathy, like a wasting disease, had brought their rebuilding programme to a standstill.

Haggai may be old, but with a vigour that defies his age, he challenges the people, stirring up afresh their desire to continue the task they had started almost twenty years before. The ruined temple was like a decayed skeleton in the city, a contamination. It was a brief but wonderfully effective ministry, perhaps for as little as four months. Should he return to our world, Haggai need not look further for his text than to the Great Sermon of Jesus: 'Seek ye first the Kingdom of God.'

The root of our problems in today's world is our obsession with materialism and our neglect of God and His commandments.

'Come back, Haggai — we need you!'

THE SOLEMN AND oft-repeated warnings of the prophets in Israel were grimly fulfilled when Jerusalem was conquered by the Babylonian army in 587 BC.

The covenant people of God had forsaken the true faith, violated their special relationship with the Lord; and in the worship of false gods had fallen far short of those standards of morality enshrined in the covenant and the commandments.

Jerusalem was virtually destroyed and the walls broken down, and the Temple of Solomon was set ablaze. At the same time many of the Jews, including those most gifted, were carried off into exile, only the poorest remaining to cultivate the land. What holy men of God like Jeremiah had predicted and described as divine judgement on a rebellious and disobedient people had surely come to pass.

Fifty years later one of the most enlightened rulers of ancient times, Cyrus, the Persian King, conquered Babylon in a spectacular victory. In the first year of his rule he was moved to proclaim a decree that the Jewish exiles should be encouraged to return to their homeland to restore the city of Jerusalem and rebuild the Temple of Solomon. It is the historian, Ezra, who records in graphic detail the magnanimous arrangements that were put into place as those 'whose heart God had moved'[1] prepared to leave and face so formidable a task. After their arrival and as soon as the returning exiles had settled — first things first — they erected an altar in the midst of the ruins of the foundations, recommencing worship and offering sacrifices.

When the foundations of the Temple were relaid, the people gathered with praise and thanksgiving and shouts of joy. However, in the midst of all the noise and exuberance, the sound of weeping could also be heard. Older priests and the heads of households could remember the former Temple, robbed of its gold, silver and bronze, the beautiful panels of cedar wood utterly consumed; and when they surveyed the appalling destruction, they cried bitterly.

It is perhaps unsurprising that after the first flush of

enthusiasm, the people lost heart and the rebuilding of the Temple ceased. Ezra faithfully records it. 'The work on the house of God in Jerusalem came to a standstill until the second year of the reign of Darius King of Persia.'[2]

Enter Haggai and his friend Zechariah, more than fifteen years after the rebuilding was recommenced. Haggai might have been a priest or a Levite and, though not all would agree, was probably an old man, perhaps one of those who was weeping when others were rejoicing. He has a message from God and in his wisdom shares it with the governor, an eminent man, Zerubbabel, and the high priest, Joshua. It was late August or early September, the time of the harvest, but all was not well. The crisis was not now because of a besieging army, but a state of moral paralysis, with economic mess and roaring inflation. Haggai can explain it all: it is because the Temple has been left in ruins and its reconstruction abandoned.

'It is not the time for the Lord's house to be built,' the people said. The words expressed their current mood.

'Not the time?' challenged the prophet. 'What do you mean, not the time?' And he continued with no thought of compromise or excuse. 'I tell you what!' he exclaimed (Haggai had not the eloquence and command of language of some of the other prophets we have met). 'You jolly well have had the time to improve your houses and panel them with wood, wood which costs the earth here in inflationary times.' And scarcely hiding his indignation or pausing for breath, he describes their economic problems in the sort of language not out of place today. 'Your harvests have failed; you're never satisfied' — and then his most telling words — 'You earn wages only to put them in a purse with holes in it! Think about it!' he thundered. 'Think about it carefully!'

We can imagine the cedar-wood merchants, going round the houses like double-glazing salesmen today. 'Buy now; pay later!' they cry, disguising their inflated prices for a scarce commodity with offers of credit. In their zeal for home improvements, the rebuilding of the Temple has been on the back burner for years and Haggai is in no doubt that the drought in its severity is God's chastisement for wrong priorities and wilful neglect.

The ever-practical prophet turned his words of reproach into a stirring challenge and call to action. '"Go up into the mountains and bring down timber and build the house of God. These are words of the Lord Almighty. He said: 'I will take pleasure in it and be honoured; I will appear in my glory.'"' Stones, of course, were plentiful, but wood was scarce in the city. Stones were memorials of the past; the wood was the promise of the future. Many of the original foundation stones remained on site, blackened by fire, but capable of renovation and therefore reusable, but the beautiful boards of cedar and cypress, many of them carved with gourds and open flowers, and the olive-wood doors of the former sanctuary were no more, their glory departed.

The prophet saw the rebuilding of the Temple as a first and necessary step to the renewal of the religious life of the people. It was the skilful diplomacy and experience of Haggai which kept Zerubbabel, the governor, and Joshua, the priest, 'on side' during these exchanges, forming a holy triumvirate of irresist-ible force and influence which evoked an immediate and spon-taneous response. 'The leaders and all the remnant of the people obeyed the voice of the Lord their God and feared before the Lord.'

How encouraged Haggai must have been to see repentance for their apathy and selfish indifference, and their neglect of their priorities! How thrilled he must have been to see the people change their attitudes and recommence the restoration work! It was a wonderful mid-September day, made memorable by another message from the Lord which stirred up the spirits of the governor, the priest and all those who volunteered their help. 'I am with you,' declares the Lord, a wonderfully re-assuring word to fan into a flame the embers of a languishing faith.

Those autumn days were filled with activity in Jerusalem.

Urgent work was needed in the orchards, vineyards and fields. It was also festival time and the observance of holy days when ceremonial took precedence over labour. Those who volunteered to rebuild the Temple faced a daunting task. Materials were in short supply; few skilled carpenters and masons, and no levies of forced labour were available. There were little groups of elderly spectators gathered round the perimeter, too old to work, but not too old to make very unfavourable comparisons of the present with the past. They had seen the former Temple in all its glory when they were children and they looked on the ruined buildings with dismay. Morale was low, nostalgia high, and the builders were already losing heart when Haggai intervened with another rousing word from God. Dismissing the pessimistic murmurings of the sightseers, he brought an upbeat and inspirational message. He addressed the leaders and all the people with an energy which surely defied his age and shamed the rest. 'Take courage,' he urged. 'Take courage. Take courage. Work, for I am with you.' His triple cry was accompanied by a reminder of their salvation history, and their deliverance from Egypt, and by an assurance that resources would be available. These were gloriously optimistic words, reaching prophetically far beyond their immediate task, to the fulfilment of God's purposes for His world.

Nostalgia is an armchair luxury. It is like a grammar lesson — the present tense, the past perfect! There could be no looking back with vain regret, but only a looking forward to a future bright with the promises of God.

The elderly prophet is in touch with God on a daily basis as his carefully-kept diary clearly shows. Two months later he receives two final messages, one to the priest, and one to the governor. The thrust of the first message is concerned with holiness. He compares contact with the garments of the priest with contact with a dead body. There is no contamination from the former, but there certainly is with the latter. To make a point in our language and culture we might use the analogy of a rotten apple in a basket of fruit; it will contaminate the good apples. Israel had been infected by too close an association with idolatry and the false gods they found in the promised land — a perpetual source of Divine anger. It is the prophet's quaint way of insisting that spiritual renewal must go hand in hand with the physical restoration of the Temple.

The second message — and the final one — is to the governor, a man of excellent pedigree and in the Royal line of David. His name is included by Matthew in his genealogy of Jesus. The Lord has chosen him for this, the highest honour; to be an ancestor of the Messiah. The signet ring was always worn on the finger of the King. The rebuilding of the Temple was to be seen as part of the process of preparation for the coming of the Messiah and the building of another temple, against which the gates of hell would not prevail.

No one can read Haggai's fascinating story without thinking of the words of Jesus in His great sermon. He warned against an obsession with material things and urged His disciples to get their priorities right. 'Seek first the kingdom of God,' He said. It is easy for us in an age of consumerism to become materialistic, to relegate spiritual matters to the second division of our programme. Our task as Christians is to build the Church with the living stones of transformed lives.

Haggai, like Barnabas of the early Church, is remembered as a great encourager, urging on the faint-hearted with positive words and warm thoughts, words of hope where there is despair, energetic words where apathy has set in, words that point to the future rather than words that recriminate over an irrecoverable past.

If Zephaniah may be regarded as a role model for the young, Haggai can be seen as a role model for the elderly. Old age is not a disease, not a time to dwell on the 'hurt of waning powers', but a time to discover how valuable is experience. The strange, eventful history of one's life is not second childishness and mere oblivion, as Shakespeare would have said, but another opportunity, not necessarily gathering stones together but, with mature wisdom, to co-ordinate Church and State, priest and governor, to help create a better world. Reminiscence may be a part-time pleasure, but the temptation to dwell in the past must be resisted. After all, as Robert Browning expressed it: 'Grow old along with me, the best is yet to be.'

When John Wesley was an old man, this is how someone described him. 'In him, old age appeared delightful, like an evening without cloud. It was impossible to observe him without wishing, "May my latter end be like this."' The same may surely be said of Haggai, whose brief prophecy is still relevant, still supremely able to encourage and inspire.

---

[1] Ezra chapter 1. [2] Ezra 4:24.

HAGGAI: STUDY GUIDE

For personal reflection and/or group discussion

1. Haggai found support from Joshua, the High Priest, and from the gover-
    nor, Zerubbabel, as he roused God's people from their apathy and half-
    heartedness.
    Does his example encourage us to challenge Church and State as we ad-
    dress the economic, social and spiritual problems of our time?

2. Is one of the perils of old age a tendency to compare the present un-
    favourably with the past?
    Does the example of Haggai help us to remedy this?

3. With reference to the mission of the end-time Church, someone has apt-
    ly said:
            'The task is great
                The team is small
                    The time is short.'
    How would you use Haggai's message to support a text like that?

4. 'Don't resent growing old; many do not have the opportunity of doing
    so.' (Anon.)
    Discuss.

5. Caleb was 40 years old when Moses sent him to spy out the land. At 85,
    with his strength undiminished, the man who 'wholly followed the Lord'
    said to Joshua:
    'Give me this mountain.'
    Inspired by Haggai's example, what mountains would you like to
    possess?

MAJOR
Themes
from
MINOR
Prophets

Malachi

The prophet of revival

A WINDOW ON MALACHI'S TIME

Imagine a fine sailing ship in the middle of the ocean. It is becalmed. It cannot proceed on its voyage because there is not the slightest breeze. When the winds were strong and the waves were high, the seamen met the challenge with enthusiasm, but now they are bored and frustrated, waiting impatiently for the weather to change.

That is a picture of God's people Israel when Malachi, God's messenger, prophesied in the middle of the fifth century BC. The Temple had been rebuilt under the inspiring leadership of Haggai and his friends. Now, however, vitality in religion was gone. It was a waiting time and the people, with a few honourable exceptions, were going through the motions, grudging in their giving, nominal and perfunctory in their worship; 'a form of godliness' without the power.

There was worse. Because of social and economic distress, the quality of the people's tithes and offerings had deteriorated to a scandal. The priests had lost all sense of vocation. They were corrupt and no longer provided the people with true instruction. Many men had entered into marriage with foreign women and begun to worship foreign gods.

Malachi's outspoken message is met with much argument and self-justification, but he will not be deflected from his condemnation of their apathy, scepticism and contempt for God's covenant and His commandments. He ignores their protests and interventions and calls for repentance and renewal. They must return to the Lord and bring their tithes and then the Lord will bless and prosper them again.

You will see how relevant the prophet's message is for today's Church, striking at the heart of nominal, easy-going Christianity. Keep the image of the ship in mind — sails but no sailing — and then use these familiar words as a prayer:

'O Breath of Life, come sweeping through us
Revive Your Church with life and power.
O Breath of Life, come cleanse, renew us,
And fit your Church to meet this hour.'

THE ANONYMOUS writer of this last little book in the Old Testament must have been inspired to call himself 'Malachi', a pseudonym which means 'My Messenger'.

If on the one hand he preferred to efface himself; on the other he would have people to be in no doubt that his message was from God — he is God's spokesman.

There is, however, another and very attractive explanation for so apt a choice. Malachi was to announce the first messenger to prepare the way for the Messiah and the ministry of Jesus. In a glowing tribute to John the Baptist, Jesus Himself explained that John was indeed the 'Elijah' of whom Malachi had prophesied, thus forging a wonderful link in the golden chain of Scripture.

Although nothing is known of the man himself, it is clear that he lived in the middle of the fifth century before Christ, a contemporary of Nehemiah and Ezra, those two stalwarts who did so much to restore the physical and spiritual fortunes of Jerusalem after the years of exile in Babylon. It was a waiting time for the people of Judah and the holy city — this closing period of the Old Testament — a time when much-needed reform was an essential preparation for the advent of the Messiah. Religious faith was dimmed and worship had degenerated to become perfunctory, nominal and sub-standard. Life was humdrum and unexciting, the service of the people grudging and unworthy; there was no vision of God, without which the people perish. What, then, did God say to His covenant people at such a time? How did they respond and in what ways are these inspired words relevant, challenging and appropriate to us in our very different world?

Malachi begins beautifully by reaffirming God's unchanging love for Israel, but the ecstasy soon becomes enigma as, in an imaginary dialogue, the people ask about the nature of His love. God's reply takes us back to the beginning and to the time when the Almighty elected to focus His love on Jacob rather than Esau (that is, Edom), a truly fascinating saga described so vividly by Obadiah. Jacob is the choice of grace alone. In old

Hebrew thought, it was either to love or to hate with nothing in between! It means a special choice of one against another, a choice made in the foreknowledge of God, which in discussion of election must be reconciled with man's free will. It is the 'amazing grace' in the popular hymn of John Newton, who in the words of his own epitaph was 'an infidel and a libertine . . . preserved, restored, pardoned and appointed to preach the faith'. God loves as a father for He has created us,[1] but He also loves as a faithful husband. He longs to be honoured by His children, His Godly offspring, and He also yearns for an unbroken relationship of faithfulness. He is a covenant-keeping God who expects reciprocal trust and obedience, a concept threaded through all the prophets.

God's message was uncompromising and severe. Instead of the honour and respect which was His due, He had been treated with contempt and not least by the priests, the spiritual leaders, on whom so much responsibility rested. The Temple had been restored through the ministry of Haggai and Zechariah, and worship had been resumed, but it was a matter of going through the motions, joyless and defiled, a form of religion without power, a reluctant duty rather than real delight. They were offering God polluted food, animals that were blind or lame, offerings that were wholly unworthy and unacceptable, which any governor would have refused out of hand and regarded as an insult! How much more the Lord of Hosts!

When the people intervened again, in uncomprehending stubbornness, the Lord explained that by their actions they had made the altar, the Lord's table, contemptible and despised. The use of the phrase 'the Lord's table' as an alternative to 'altar' is to reach once again beyond the inter-testamental years to the upper room of the last supper.

The Lord had no pleasure in their worship, for they were cheating Him or, in Malachi's memorable phrase, 'robbing God'. He would not accept such offerings and, as if to express the divine yearning for a time when the faith would spread throughout the whole world, God declared: '"From the rising of the sun to its setting my name is great among the nations."'[2]

The priests of Israel were singled out for special condemnation because they had refused to listen to God or take to heart the honour of His name. Instead of a blessing they must bear a curse and were despised and humiliated. How far short had they fallen from the standards set for Levi in the original covenant of priesthood — a covenant of life and peace, a service characterized by fear and awe, a ministry of true instruction, knowledge and uprightness! Those priests had violated their sacred office and betrayed their vocation, causing many to stumble and fall away.

Those who are in leadership among God's people today are also highly privileged; they are the custodians of the truth which is to be proclaimed fearlessly and faithfully. They must also be examples in their life-style and of blameless character, for leadership is a noble task, which, like marriage, must not be undertaken carelessly, lightly or selfishly, but reverently and responsibly.

Like an unfaithful wife who had broken her marriage vows, Israel had broken faith with a loving God. Indeed, many had become involved in mixed marriages with the 'daughter of a foreign god' and then had had the nerve to shed crocodile tears in emotional outbursts because their inferior sacrifices had not been accepted! 'Guard yourself and do not break faith' is a divine admonition which still rings true in the church today. Unholy alliances in human as well as spiritual relationships are dangerous and destructive, an unequal yoke to be avoided at all costs. God is a God of justice.

The message of the prophet modulates from tones of reproach and rebuke to the brighter music of reformation and renewal. Instead of recriminations about the failure of Israel to keep the Old Covenant, we see intimations of a New Covenant as preparations begin for the coming Messiah. Who will be ready for this momentous event? Who will endure that day and stand before the Lord when He comes suddenly to His Temple?

What is so urgently needed is 'the refiner's fire' to purify God's people in preparation for that great day. As someone who knew the Holy Land well explained it, 'The beauty of this picture is that the refiner looks into the open furnace and knows that the process of purifying is complete and the dross all burnt away when he can see his image plainly reflected in the molten metal.' In our invocation of the Holy Spirit, we may sing;

> 'Come as the fire to purge our hearts
> Like sacrificial flame;
> Let our whole soul an offering be
> To our Redeemer's name.'

Malachi is anxious that Israel will be ready, a holy people whose offerings will again be worthy and acceptable, but he is also aware that all who do not repent and turn away from their wicked ways will be swiftly judged. The unchanging covenant-keeping God calls His people to return to Him and repair the broken relationship between them, and yet again this man of God who speaks God's words imagines the people intervening. 'How are we to return?' they ask, and continue, 'You say we have robbed You. How do we rob You?' It was a naïve pretence of innocence in people who knew perfectly well in what ways they had disappointed a loving Father. 'Bring full tithes into the store-house,' God said. 'Prove Me, put Me to the test.' His words were followed with an extravagant promise: 'I will open the windows of Heaven and pour out upon you so much blessing that there will not be enough room to receive it.'

All of this is seen by our messenger as Advent preparation. As the clarion call for repentance dies away, we hear other voices as those who now fear the Lord speak to one another. They experience a new sense of belonging, as a treasured possession of a faithful God of unchanging and steadfast love. Malachi heralds the coming day of the Lord; it will be like a burning fire to consume all evil-doers, but, in contrast, it will be a glorious sunrise for all who honour the Lord. In his famous last words, Israel is reminded of Moses and the commandments that were the conditions of the covenant entered into at Horeb (Sinai). Then there is the dramatic announcement that Elijah will come to prepare the way of the Lord. It is surely no coincidence that when Jesus was transfigured on the mountain, and when His face shone like the sun, Moses and Elijah appeared and talked to Him. It was as they came down from the mountain that the disciples reminded their master of the prophecy that Elijah must come. 'Elijah has already come,' said Jesus, and there was no doubt in their minds that He was speaking of John the Baptist![3]

Of all the minor prophets, none is more challenging to the Christian Church than 'My Messenger' Malachi. His is still an Advent message and a call to readiness for that great day when our Lord returns. We do not know the day nor the hour when this will be. There is always the danger that our worship may become routine, cold and nominal rather than spontaneous, sweetly fresh and sacrificial. It is so easy to become like the Laodicean church to whom John wrote, neither cold nor hot, but lukewarm. We need to think creatively about worship, but, equally, to express in our daily lives those attitudes which are consistent and compatible with true devotion. The power of our religious experience is the power to enhance, beautify and transform our lives, thus to glorify the Lord in body and spirit by our worship and service and so reflect the image of Jesus.

---

[1] Mal. 2:10. [2] Mal. 1:11. [3] Matt. 17:9-13.

MALACHI: STUDY GUIDE

For personal reflection and/or group discussion

1. Discuss how the prophet describes God's covenant with Levi with
    reference to leadership in today's Church (see Mal. 2:4-7). Remember
    Levi was the priestly tribe.
    Is the Christian ministry a career or a vocation?
    Does the clergy of today's Church deserve any of Malachi's strictures?

2. Among the letters to the seven churches in Asia in the Book of
    Revelation is the letter to Laodicea (Rev. 3:14-22).
    In what ways does this letter parallel the message of Malachi?

3. Why is it that in so many congregations in all denominations, there is
    only a loyal core, a 'faithful few', who 'fear the Lord and speak often to
    one another' (Mal. 3:16, 17)?
    How can the Church as a whole be set on fire?
    How do the 'faithful few' become the faithful many?

4. In commending loyalty and faithfulness in marriage, Malachi condemns
    those who betray the mutual trust between husband and wife. 'I hate
    divorce,' saith the Lord (Mal. 2:16).
    How do these words relate to relationships now?
    Has God's attitude to divorce changed?

5. When rabbis read Malachi in the synagogue, they read to the end of
    chapter 4, verse 6, and then reread the preceding verses.
    Can you think why?
    You may like to compare this last word 'curse' in the Old Testament with
    the last word 'grace' in the New. As a matter of interest, see the last two
    verses in Isaiah 66:23, 24 and Lamentations 5:21, 22, which are also
    reversed.
    Can you give reasons for this?

MAJOR
Themes
from
MINOR
Prophets

Joel
The prophet of Pentecost

A WINDOW ON JOEL'S TIME

If you search for the prophet Joel in the index of your Bible, you will find him among the eighth century prophets whom we met when our journey began. He is chaperoned between Hosea and Amos. You will be surprised to discover that we now meet him at almost the end and you deserve an explanation! There is a consensus of opinion that his stirring words were uttered at the end of the fifth century, around four hundred years before Christ. The book may be one of the briefest in the Old Testament, but it is one of the most disturbing.

The scene is Jerusalem and the season is Pentecost, the Feast which comes some fifty days after the Passover. The people are expected to bring sacrifices in gratitude for the harvest, but they come to the Temple empty-handed. Their fields and vineyards, orchards and gardens have been devastated by an enormous plague of locusts. Great swarms of these voracious insects have come from the deserts of Arabia to darken the sky and devour everything in sight. Everything is perished. It is an historical event which Joel describes in his forceful and artistic eloquence. It is, however, the judgement of God, but it is not too late to return to the Lord in repentance. He calls for sackcloth, for brokenness and tears; there must be a national day of prayer and the Lord will answer. The rain will fall in abundance, the fields will be green once more, the trees will bear fruit, the barns will be full and the wine vats overflowing. There will be offerings for Pentecost after all!

Joel reaches the high point of his sermon with the prophecy of the outpouring of the Holy Spirit, which Peter saw so dramatically fulfilled when the Spirit came upon the disciples of Jesus. He is by no means exhausted, however, but goes on to speak of 'the day of the Lord' in vivid pictures of future glory.

'THINK OF A world without any flowers,
Think of a wood without any trees,
Think of a sky without any sunshine,
Think of the air without any breeze.'

These words of a modern hymn would have suited the mood of the prophet Joel. As Pentecost, the feast of ingathering, drew near, the time of the harvest when the people were expected to bring the first-fruits of field and vineyard as an offering, there was nothing but gloom and despair in Jerusalem. A great plague of locusts, an unstoppable black flood of voracious insects, wave after wave, had swept across the land. They had eaten the wheat and barley harvest; the vines and fig trees had dried up and withered. The prophet was obviously describing an historical event, offering a prophetic interpretation of a contemporary disaster.

'The joy of mankind is withered away,' Joel cries. No wonder the temple priests are in mourning and the farmers in despair. Such equally destructive natural disasters are not unknown in our world, though we now have more sophisticated ways of controlling such plagues.

In an excess of modesty, Joel tells us nothing about himself; and, unlike some other prophets, he puts down no historical markers to tell us when he lived. The scribes who compiled the Old Testament set him among the eighth century prophets, Hosea and Amos. However, it is now generally believed that he preached the word of the Lord about 400BC. The Temple is functioning, the city walls have been repaired and there are quotations and references to the earlier men of God whose stories we have already heard. Joel might have been a Temple prophet; he certainly felt strongly that Temple sacrifices were the divinely-appointed means of fellowship with God, festivals and feasts an essential part of worship. Joel is a communicator with great passion and artistic skill. With vivid words he presents the disaster as an act of God and as a parable of divine judgement. Powerful armies have invaded the land in the past and may do so again. It is time for people to wake up, to put on the sackcloth of true repentance and declare a holy fast, time for a national day of prayer. Elders, priests and ministers are summoned to hear the prophet speak of the 'day of the Lord'. 'Here this,' he cries. 'Listen; none of you can remember anything like this. You must be sure to pass on this message to your children and grandchildren.'

It is a terrifying message that Joel delivers: the day of the Lord is dreadful, who can endure it? It is close at hand, a day of darkness and gloom. It is obvious that he sees the successive defeats that have befallen the people of Judah and Jerusalem at the hands of powerful enemies as divine retribution for infidelity, apostasy, idolatry and moral decadence. These invading armies have been 'instruments of chastisement' to God's covenant people.

However, all is not lost, nor is all hope abandoned, for Joel also sees the possibilities of recovery, restoration and renewal and the eventual victory of righteousness in the kingdom of God. His call for repentance is spoken with great tenderness in contrast with the vehemence and stridency of his earlier utterances. 'Return to Me . . . rend your hearts and not your garments. Tearing your clothes is not enough . . . let your broken heart show your sorrow.' There are deeply-moving images also: 'Mourn like a virgin for the bridegroom in her youth. Like a girl who mourns for the man she was going to marry, the highest hopes of a loving and fruitful relationship dashed and devastated.' Who would not be moved by such words as these? He describes a God whose anger is only the graver countenance of His love, a God who is merciful as well as righteous, patient and unfailing in His steadfast love.

The prophet's trumpet has a clear and certain sound as he calls upon the whole community to gather together in assembly. The whole family is to come, even the newborn babies and the newly married. They are to call on the Lord to spare them and remove the reproach of defeat for His name's sake.

In memorable and beautiful words the Lord replies, using a famous phrase that has become almost a proverb, "'I will restore to you the years that the locusts have eaten.'"[1] Cereal offerings and wine offerings will again be available. "'Be not afraid, O land; be glad and rejoice. God will send you the autumn rains in righteousness and pledge that all will know He is Lord in the midst of Israel.'"[2]

We now reach the pinnacle of the amazing book when the prophet utters a Pentecostal prophecy to be gloriously fulfilled as, after the ascension of the risen Christ, the promised Spirit would come to the early Christian Church. The Messiah has come and afterwards, "'I will pour out My Spirit on all flesh.'"[3] Peter explains the remarkable phenomenon of Spirit-filled believers as the fulfilment of Joel's words, but, of course, his imagery reaches far beyond that wonderful post-resurrection experience to 'the day of the Lord'. Between the two there stretched a long day of opportunity, when the Gospel of salvation will be preached throughout the whole world. At Pentecost another great harvest is envisaged, greater than the thanksgiving for the fruits of the earth. The Lord of the harvest would send His labourers forth. The gifts of the Spirit would be bestowed on all who believe as well as the fruits of the Spirit, which Paul described of love, joy and peace, patience, kindness, goodness, faithfulness, gentleness and self-control.[4]

The theme of judgement is one which Joel does not easily put behind him. Even as he predicts that God will restore the fortunes of Judah and Jerusalem, he is also convinced that God is judge of all the earth. Nations which have afflicted God's people Israel will themselves be afflicted. Moreover, the wrath of God will be revealed against all the nations when great wickedness will eventually be judged.

His final words reach forward in ecstasy to a glorious future. Jerusalem will become a holy city where God will dwell and all men will know Him. It will be pardoned of all guilt in a day of prosperity when the Lord will be a refuge for His people. The great divine intervention of God is seen in the coming to earth of the Messiah and finally when Christ ushers in His glorious kingdom.

This strange, near-anonymous mystic is long-since dead, but still he speaks. Nations forsake God at their peril for they will be judged and God's purposes for our world will not be finally frustrated. The infallible morality of the Almighty must be proclaimed and the call to repentance is a trumpet call that must still sound out, loud and clear. Divine retribution is always available. God's character is the perfect balance of justice and love, judgement and mercy.

There is a very personal word here also. How many people, looking back over their lives, can speak with regret of the years the locusts have eaten — locust plagues of half-heartedness, insincerity, false teaching and unbelief. The call is for a change of heart, a time to repent in brokenness, but not to leave a vacuum, rather that the emptiness may indeed be filled with the fruits of the Spirit and a harvest of righteousness, which we may bring back to the Lord as a Pentecostal offering.

If the words of the hymn which were quoted at the beginning expressed the mood of Joel then at the end we may encourage him to join in the refrain:

> 'We thank you, Lord, for flowers and trees and sunshine,
> We thank you, Lord, and praise Your Holy name.'

---

[1] Joel 2:25. [2] Joel 2:23. [3] Joel 2:28. [4] Gal. 5:22.

JOEL: STUDY GUIDE

For personal reflection and/or group discussion

1. In times of national crisis, is there a place for a Day of Prayer?
    Can you think of occasions in recent history when such a day has been,
    or should have been, observed?

2. Among the most memorable of his words, the prophet Joel said, 'Rend
    your hearts and not your garments.' (Joel 2:13.)
    What do you think these words mean?

3. 'The years which the locusts have eaten.' (Joel 2:25.)
    Can you relate these words to any experience of your own?

4. The longing for 'an outpouring of the Holy Spirit' is often expressed in
    today's Church.
    Can Pentecost (Acts chapter 2) be repeated and how would you describe
    the work of the Holy Spirit
    a) in the life of the individual and
    b) in the corporate life of the Church?

5. Is there a conflict between God's love and God's justice?
    Do we sometimes over-emphasize one at the expense of the other?

MAJOR
Themes
from
MINOR
Prophets

Zechariah

'The King is coming'

A WINDOW ON ZECHARIAH'S TIME

It may seem perverse that in our meeting with the minor prophets we have left Zechariah to the last. After all, he was a contemporary of Haggai and helped that great 'Encourager' to motivate the returned exiles to complete the rebuilding of the Temple. The reason for this is not alphabetical — in spite of his name! Nor is it historical. Rather the reason is prophetical, as, in the grand manner, he speaks of the arrival of the Messiah and portrays Him as the Lord and King over all the earth; He who is ultimately victorious when all the nations will come to Jerusalem as the centre of true worship, a city of great joy and a home for all!

Zechariah speaks of God's anger as others have done and repeats an urgent call for repentance and a return to the Lord. He sees the catastrophes of previous centuries as a consequence of Israel's broken covenant and evil ways. He is a student of history, striving to understand how God is working out His purposes. Surely Israel has received the punishment it deserved, but the nation will be purged of all her sins in preparation for the arrival of the Messiah.

Zechariah's prophecy provides us with a glorious climax to the Old Testament in the way that the Revelation of John does in the New Testament. The two books are similar, featuring visions and images which are difficult to interpret, 'enigmas wrapped in mysteries'. They present a challenge to our 'little grey cells' as fascinating, as fulfilling. We must be on the alert as we read of words that relate to the suffering Messiah, the King who rides in lowly pomp to die outside the city walls, but equally of the King who is coming to reign. Zechariah would urge us to be ready, so that when the King comes we may meet Him and greet Him with confidence and joy.

'GRANDPAS ARE delightful things; they date back to the last century. They live in their own funny world where time seems to go backwards. Grandfather cares for everything, everything but himself.'

The words come in a highly entertaining book on our coffee table, written by grandchildren for their grandparents.

Zechariah would have loved that book for it is often supposed that his father died when he was young and his grandfather, Iddo, brought him up. He almost certainly came back with him from Babylon, accompanying Zerubbabel, the governor, and Joshua, the priest. His grandfather would have taught him the sorry history of their nation; and since he was among the chief priests, he would also have given him a thorough knowledge of their spiritual heritage as the chosen people of God. As a young man he had been carefully groomed and educated to be both priest and prophet. His name means 'The Lord remembers', which may seem apt and appropriate as his fascinating story unfolds.

Zechariah was contemporary with Haggai whom we concluded (we may be wrong!) was an old man. They were obviously friends and shared the same enthusiasm for the rebuilding of the Temple in Jerusalem. His prophecy is the longest of the books of the minor prophets, but it must be said that the second part (chapters 9-14) is so different from the first part that it is usually thought to have been written by another person at a later time. However, it is obvious from the text that the young prophet has a great acquaintance with all parts of the Old Testament. None of the prophets is quoted so frequently in the gospels in the New Testament. He is a man of dreams and visions who added stained-glass windows of colour, light and symbols to the prophetic story.

Many of his phrases are memorable and have become part of our vocabulary. However, this obscure piece of Old Testament literature is demanding to read, as are parts of Daniel, Ezekiel and, pre-eminently, the Book of Revelation.

Luther had a high regard for Zechariah and called his work

'the quintessence of the prophets'; he certainly seems to sum up the prophetic message and catches the echoes of all that his predecessors have spoken. He looks at the spiritual needs of the world and at world events to see if he can understand how God is working out His purpose. His book is full of the struggle towards peace on earth and goodwill to men. How will God's kingdom be established and evil powers overthrown? There are moments when Zechariah is overwhelmed with gloom as evil seems to gain the upper hand and as God's servants are eliminated by wicked men, but his ringing confidence is reflected in a key phrase — a proclamation — 'The Lord is King'. He is visited by the angel of the Lord, and the angelic choir singing the Gloria.

Zechariah begins with the anger of God, an anger directed against 'their forefathers' who had refused to listen to the voices of the prophets and suffered in consequence. To his present audience, his call is for repentance: 'Return to Me and I will return to you.' The people recognized that their forebears got what they deserved for their ways and practices; as they now repent and turn in obedience to the Lord, they are to hear kind and comforting words. Like Haggai, he encourages them to press on with the rebuilding of the Temple, and shares his vision of the glories of the Messianic kingdom that will, in due time, be fulfilled.

In a single night Zechariah had no fewer than eight visions, strangely mysterious with touches of vivid imagery. An angel is there as an interpreter, though, at first, the prophet might have been puzzled as we are as to what the visions mean!

Let us imagine we have made Zechariah's visions into a video so that we can see these brilliant images, animated and in full colour. Do not even ask what they mean — not for the moment. In media language we might be tempted to say, 'I'm sorry; I haven't a clue.'

At first, the small screen is filled with horses and their riders, patrolling the world. The picture fades and reappears to show four horns which are seen to be destroyed by the hammers of four craftsmen. This is followed by a surveyor, measuring out the city, and then, strangely, a priest who first appears in filthy clothes, but is stripped of his unseemly garments and robed in rich vestments. The priest is, of course, Joshua, and in front of him is a stone on which are seven eyes. Then there is a solid gold lampstand with a bowl on top and seven lights on it. There is an olive tree on either side. We are more mystified and confused then ever. It is 'curiouser and curiouser' as we wait in a wonderland to see what else will appear.

Now we see a flying scroll, thirty feet long and half as wide; and, more bizarre still, a woman in a basket who is lifted up by two women with wings. Finally, in a grand climax, four chariots appear, drawn by horses of differing colours: red, black, white and dappled. They emerge between two mountains of bronze, and seem to be charging through the whole earth. The pictures are a marvel, but what on earth do they mean? We'll turn up the sound and see if the angel interpreter can help us. We listen intently, not to miss a word as the angel speaks:

'"The horse riders you saw in the beginning have completed a reconnaissance of the earth and found the whole world at rest and in peace. The Lord Almighty will now be gracious to Jerusalem, with the same blessings of peace and prosperity. At the same time," the angel continues, '"those enemies who humiliated and afflicted God's people will themselves be destroyed. Israel is the 'apple of God's eye' and Jerusalem, a 'city without walls', will become a home for all, restored amid great shouts of joy."'

The vision of Joshua in his filthy garments is more accessible to us, as the angel continues his interpretation. Israel will be purged of all her sin and uncleanness and clothed in garments of salvation and robes of righteousness, as if prepared for the coming Messiah who is referred to as 'the branch'. The gold lampstand (also a more familiar image) represents the congregation as a spiritual light in a dark world, encouraged by the governor and priest, symbolized by the olive trees. There are famous words to explain: '"Not by might, nor by power, but by my spirit," saith the Lord.' We need to pause and reflect before our guide concludes:

'"The flying scroll carries a stern warning for all evil doers to read, and God's condemnation of sin, while the woman in the basket is sin and idolatry personified and is justly removed to Babylon, the place of exile. The grand finale of horse-drawn chariots is a reminder that God is in control. The dawn is breaking and the prophet's long night of trauma is ending. So there will be a new dawn when rest and peace will cover the whole earth."' As if to confirm how the glorious Kingdom will come, Joshua, the priest, is crowned as a symbol of the One who will come, both Priest and King, the Messiah, spoken of again as the Branch. What a night for Zechariah to remember, and what a wonderful and mysterious experience for us! We may want to run the video tape again and again.

Two years passed before Zechariah received another message from the Lord. Questions about fasting were raised, but the prophet explained in no uncertain terms that justice, mercy and compassion, social awareness and a life-style marked by love, truth and peace were of far greater importance than rituals. Indeed, in the future, fasts will become festivals when the Lord comes into the city of Jerusalem which He loves. Zechariah paints a beautiful picture of very old people, needing a cane for support, who will sit contentedly in the street, while the boys and girls play. Everything will prosper and no one need be afraid. Other peoples from other nations will encourage one another to come to Jerusalem and share the blessings, because they have heard that God is with His people. It is the promise of a glorious future.

It is always pointed out that the second half of this unique piece of Old Testament literature is so very different from that which preceded it, that either it was the work of someone else, or, as I prefer to suggest, it was written by the same prophet at a much later date. Judgement is pronounced on neighbouring nations, but the hope of Jerusalem is in the coming of the

Messiah. The prophet's words are the 'Palm Sunday' prophecy; 'Rejoice greatly, O daughter of Zion. Behold your King comes, gentle and riding on a donkey.'[1] The people suffer for want of a shepherd. The Messiah is the Good Shepherd who must first lay down His life for the sheep and be sold for thirty pieces of silver. A fountain is opened for sin and uncleanness which is a figure often used of the cross of Jesus while the Master Himself quoted the prophet's words. '"Smite the shepherd and the sheep will be scattered."'[2] 'At last, the Lord will be King over all the earth — one Lord — and His name is the only name.'[3]

It is out of kindness that we have not dwelt too deeply on this latter part of Zechariah's prophecy and with no disrespect to a man of genius, grace and spirituality. Now that we have opened up his pages, what indeed is his message for us? It is a message of confident hope which nothing can quench, a light at eventide that cannot be extinguished. The night is far spent, to use Paul's words; the day is at hand. It is time to cast off the works of darkness, time to prepare for the great day of the Lord. It is time for pure worship, without hypocrisy, acknowledging Jesus as King in our own lives. It is a call to be awake, alert and ready, watching and waiting for the dawn of God's new world. 'Lift up your heads for your redemption draweth nigh.'[4]

And finally — a word which preachers say and do not always mean — Zechariah may have another lesson to teach us. When we are reading esoteric material like much of his prophecy, we may not always understand, but faith transcends understanding. As St Anselm, the Archbishop of Canterbury in the eleventh century, expressed it in a classical statement, 'I do not seek to understand that I may believe, but I believe that I may understand.' In our spiritual pilgrimage, it is a rule worth remembering!

---

[1] Zech. 9:9. [2] Zech. 13:7; Matt. 26:31. [3] Zech. 14:9. [4] Luke 21:28.

ZECHARIAH: STUDY GUIDE

For personal reflection and/or group discussion

1. Can you describe the difference between 'believing' and 'understanding'?
    Is there such a thing as 'blind faith'?

2. How does the world in which we live compare with the world of the
    prophets? Why is the call to repentance so urgent today and how can this
    call be delivered? Is today's Church providing an answer to the problems
    in societies throughout the world?

3. If it were possible to have only one of the prophets we have met for a
    weekend in your home, whom would you choose, and for what reason?

4. You are encouraged to 'cut open' these remarkable little books and read
    them. These studies have been written not for preachers who require
    commentaries, but for the average Christian who loves the Bible and
    wants to enjoy all of it. Have they succeeded?

5. 'Most of us today are afraid of denouncing evil for fear of being called
    intolerant.' . . .
    — 'We are not allowed to have definite values of right and wrong.'
    'We are frightened of sharing our faith with a fellow human being for fear
    of interfering in his private beliefs.'
    (Words of J. B. Phillips in his preface to his book *Four Prophets*.)
    Do you agree with these strictures, and in what ways do the prophets
    challenge us?

A final thought.
Do read through these prophetic books at a sitting, preferably aloud and
with others. You will enjoy the richness of the language even if some of the
meaning still eludes you.

MAJOR
Themes
from
MINOR
Prophets

An
epilogue

A legacy of
unchanging
values

'THE BOOKS THAT prophets write live after them; their sermons are often interred with their bones.' With more apologies to Shakespeare for misusing his words again, we salute these twelve holy men of God who in their wisdom recorded their prophecies in writing. As we cut open these previously unread pages of the Old Testament, it is as though they have appeared, one by one, upon the stage of our lives to read their inspired words once more. We have been able to lose ourselves in their wonderful minds, marvel at their eloquence, admire their courage and listen to their analysis of the world in which they lived. They have given us a vision of a God of power and authority, yet a God of unchanging and steadfast love. They have exposed the waywardness and wickedness of the human race, despairing of man's disobedience of the moral law, yet always signposting the road to recovery and reconciliation. They have described in vivid images the catastrophes of history and have shown how men who have the free will to make choices live to face the unavoidable consequences of their decisions and reap what they have sown. However, these prophets were never men to lose heart and believed in the ultimate victory of righteousness and the future glory of God's kingdom. Hope which 'springs eternal' was ever the hallmark of their messages.

Is it not true that though they have long since died, yet they still speak to our generation? Are we now ready to give a verdict on the relevance to our situation, when godlessness prevails and anxieties for the future deepen almost by the hour? In the world's despair and turmoil, what is God saying now?

The revelation of God in these prophecies has lost none of its completeness and power. God is still on the throne. The beautifully-balanced portrait of the Almighty, His everlasting love and uncompromising holiness, His infinite wisdom and incorruptible justice, His righteous anger, yet with the grief of a broken-hearted father, is as vivid and unfading as when it was originally presented by these remarkable men.

Let us imagine that we are on the mountain of Trans-figuration with Jesus in our midst. He cherished all the words the prophets had spoken and interpreted them to His disciples in His resurrection. Let us ask the Master to recall the 'Twelve' one by one to give us just a word or two for our generation. After all, He did call Moses and Elijah to join Him on the holy mountain, when Peter, James and John witnessed His majesty and when the prophetic word was made more sure.[5]

Hosea is first to appear and pleads for family love, a love to the uttermost, and also has a word for the backslider in need of healing and restoration.

Amos is next with a passionate plea for social holiness and justice, with a bishop's bias towards the poor.

Micah is too modest to remind us of his prophecy concerning the birth of Jesus and is content to encourage us to walk humbly with our God.

Jonah has a slightly apologetic look on his face as one who is none too proud of his record, but he has learnt much since his famous second chance. He speaks of a love of God which 'is broader than the measures of man's mind,' of a mercy 'like the wideness of the sea' and 'a kindness in His justice, which is more than liberty'. He knows now that there is a 'welcome for the sinner . . . mercy with the Saviour' and 'healing in His blood'. (Frederick W. Faber.)

Nahum is brief. 'Be angry and sin not', but in case we have the wrong impression of him, he quickly reminds us of his other words — 'The Lord cares for those who trust in Him.'

Habakkuk speaks with tenderness, because he understands more than most the perplexities of human experience and how often the questioning cry comes to our lips in life's mysteries, 'Why me, Lord . . . ?' 'You will understand . . . not now, but one day', he replies with such comforting words.

Obadiah warns us again about those roots of bitterness that are so damaging to the quality of life and those memories which, if unhealed, rob us of our peace of mind.

Zephaniah has words of encouragement for those who are young to stir up gifts which the Lord has given them.

Haggai has words for the elderly, but also insists, as ever, that we lay up treasure in heaven and not upon the earth. 'Put God first,' he says.

Joel appears with a charismatic flourish and his words, as we expected, have echoes of Pentecost.

Malachi seems to have lost none of his earnestness and severity. 'Don't forget tithes' — he assumes we remember his original message — and continues, 'Let your worship and service be whole-hearted, sincere and sacrificial.'

The twelfth man, **Zechariah** appears last but by no means least. We await his message with eager anticipation and he does not disappoint us! 'The King is coming,' he cries. 'His feet shall stand upon the Mount of Olives . . . . The Lord will be King over the whole earth.' The other prophets have remained to hear this triumphant climax and shout, in unison, 'Hallelujah'; but the prophet has not quite finished. 'Be ready; you do not know the day nor the hour when the King will come.'

They are about to leave us, with Jesus, but Habakkuk, music master, steps out in front. 'Let's have a song as a grand finale,' he shouts, and they all agree. It is a song we have already sung on our journey, but we are thrilled to sing it again.

'Ends of the earth, see the salvation of our God,
Jesus is Lord, is Lord,
Before the nations, He has bared His holy arm,
Our God reigns, our God reigns.'

The prophets have gone, but their inspiring books remain, and we will want to read them again, several chapters at a time, to get the feel and sweep of the prophets' minds.

As we descend the mountain to meet the real world, perhaps like Moses, although we shall be unaware of it, the skin of our faces will surely shine, and our hearts be filled with thanks to God,

' . . . whose word was written
In the Bible's sacred page,
Record of the revelation
Showing God to every age.'

---

[5] 2 Peter 1:16-19.